BACHELORS

OCTOBER Books

Rosalind Krauss, Annette Michelson, Yve-Alain Bois, Benjamin H. D. Buchloh, Hal Foster, Denis Hollier, and Silvia Kolbowski, editors

Broodthaers, edited by Benjamin H. D. Buchloh

AIDS: Cultural Analysis/Cultural Activism, edited by Douglas Crimp

Aberrations, by Jurgis Baltrušaitis

Against Architecture: The Writings of Georges Bataille, by Denis Hollier
Painting as Model, by Yve-Alain Bois

The Destruction of Tilted Arc: Documents, edited by Clara Weyergraf-Serra and Martha Buskirk

The Woman in Question, edited by Parveen Adams and Elizabeth Cowie

Techniques of the Observer: On Vision and Modernity in the Nineteenth Century, by Jonathan Crary

The Subjectivity Effect in Western Literary Tradition: Essays toward the Release of Shakespeare's Will, by Joel Fineman

Looking Awry: An Introduction to Jacques Lacan through Popular Culture, by Slavoj Žižek

Cinema, Censorship, and the State: The Writings of Nagisa Oshima, by Nagisa Oshima

The Optical Unconscious, by Rosalind E. Krauss

Gesture and Speech, by André Leroi-Gourhan

Compulsive Beauty, by Hal Foster

Continuous Project Altered Daily: The Writings of Robert Morris, by Robert Morris

Read My Desire: Lacan against the Historicists, by Joan Copjec

Fast Cars, Clean Bodies: Decolonization and the Reordering of French Culture, by Kristin Ross

Kant after Duchamp, by Thierry de Duve

The Duchamp Effect, edited by Martha Buskirk and Mignon Nixon

The Return of the Real: The Avant-Garde at the End of the Century, by Hal Foster

OCTOBER: *The Second Decade, 1986–1996,* edited by Rosalind Krauss, Annette Michelson, Yve-Alain Bois, Benjamin H. D. Buchloh, Hal Foster, Denis Hollier, and Silvia Kolbowski

Infinite Regress: Marcel Duchamp 1910–1941, by David Joselit

Caravaggio's Secrets, by Leo Bersani and Ulysse Dutoit

Scenes in a Library: Reading the Photograph in the Book, 1843–1875, by Carol Armstrong

Neo-Avantgarde and Culture Industry: Essays on European and American Art from 1965 to 1975, by Benjamin H. D. Buchloh

Bachelors, by Rosalind Krauss

BACHELORS

ROSALIND E. KRAUSS

OCTOBER

THE MIT PRESS
CAMBRIDGE, MASSACHUSETTS
LONDON, ENGLAND

This book was set in Bembo by Graphic Composition, Inc.

Printed and bound in the United States of America.

Library of Congress Cataloging-in-Publication Data

Krauss, Rosalind E.
    Bachelors / Rosalind Krauss.
        p.   cm.
    "An OCTOBER book."
    Includes bibliographical references and index.
    ISBN 0-262-11239-6 (hc : alk. paper)
    1. Feminism and the arts.   2. Originality in art.   3. Surrealism—Influence.   4. Women artists—Psychology.   I. Title.
    NX180.F4K73   1999
    704'.042—dc21   98-40301
                                                                  CIP

Contents

1
————

CLAUDE CAHUN AND DORA MAAR: BY WAY OF INTRODUCTION

I will open with an intellectual itinerary: the story of my own relation to surrealism which began as I, a young art historian and critic, was wrestling with the problem of the development of modern sculpture. This was in the 1960s and so the "problem" as I had inherited it in those years was mainly posed in terms of questions of style. Given what I saw, however, as the consistent choice of surrealist sculptors to appropriate the dominant stylistic option of closed, monolithic form and to transform Brancusi's ovoids or Maillol's archaic fragments or Moore's impassive boulders into a collection of cages and bottles and pieces of furniture, I found myself converting these stylistic adaptations into vehicles of expression. For with these elements surrealist sculpture seemed to have devised an insistent vocabulary that turned on the thematic of the incarceration of the female body and the imaginative projection of violence against it.[1]

In making this analysis I was, of course, moving within the tide of what was developing at the end of the sixties in the work of a feminist critic like Xavière Gauthier and would swell by the middle of the eighties into the flood of a generally held feminist consensus that surrealism, as a movement organized and dominated by men, was deeply misogynist.[2] If Gauthier had begun by tracing sadism toward women as the persistent thematic of surrealist imagery, analyzing it as a defense against male castration anxiety, the blanket notion of surrealist

Constantin Brancusi, *Torso of a Young Man,* ca. 1916. Wood, Philadelphia Mueum of Art, Louise and Walter Arensberg Collection.

René Magritte, *Femme-bouteille,* 1940 or 1941. Oil on claret bottle, 11 1/2 inches. Private collection, New York.

---

exploitation of women—whether actual, as in the case of the real-life Nadja recorded by André Breton in his book that bears her name, or phantasmatic, as in the dismembered dolls of Hans Bellmer or the pornographic rendering of violation in a work like Bataille's *Story of the Eye*—quickly became a fixed characterization of the movement by younger scholars, both male and female. Celebrated in collections such as the 1990 *Surrealism and Women,* this now operates as what Jane Austen (with a deliberate wink at her readers) might have called "a truth universally acknowledged."[3]

By the mid-1970s, my own experience of surrealist sculpture had undergone a change, however, as I began to realize the importance of the paradigm put in place by Giacometti's surrealist work of the early 1930s. Conceiving of the sculptural object on the model of the horizontal game board—Chinese checkers, pinballs, chess—Giacometti had profoundly altered the parameters of sculpture by folding the work into what had previously been seen as "merely" its pedestal. The twofold result of this move was, first, to make the representational field of the sculpture continuous with the real world—rather than lifted "above" or "beyond" it—and, second, to stress the transactional nature of this lowered, horizontalized object, which, like the pieces in a game of checkers, not only elicits an interaction on the part of the player(s) but locates the state of play within the temporal unfolding of the game itself.[4]

That this paradigm, invented within the field of surrealism, would have a crucial afterlife in postminimalist sculpture, whether that be earthworks, process art, or institution-critical interventions, made it all the more imperative in my eyes to move beyond received notions about surrealism itself. At the level of style there was, as I said, the unshakable "truth" that surrealism had contributed nothing to the twentieth century's history of form; while at the level of content its contribution was seen as limited to a thematics of misogyny. Since both these positions now seemed wholly inaccurate, I was glad to accept the Museum of Modern Art's invitation to contribute an essay on Giacometti for the catalogue of its "'Primitivism' and 20th Century Art" exhibition. For I had a hunch that the relation Giacometti's work forged between the board-game paradigm and tribal art might prove illuminating for analyzing the larger stakes in the shift I saw surrealist sculpture announcing.

The breakthrough to my problem came in the form of Giacometti's precise point of entry into the avant-garde, which marked the fact that before he was taken up by André Breton in 1930, he had been integrated by Michel Leiris into the circle connected to the magazine *Documents* led by Georges Bataille, a circle composed of renegade surrealists. Thoroughly ignored by the Giacometti literature as a factor of any real importance, this connection seemed, on the contrary, to yield an extraordinary harvest of conceptual issues that not only went far to account for Giacometti's choices in constructing an art that mainline surrealism would soon enthusiastically claim as its own but also generated analytic categories for understanding other parts of surrealist production that had hitherto been recalcitrant to explanation.

The most general of these categories—or terms of analysis—comes from Bataille's lapidary "Dictionary" entry devoted to the word *formless* that he published in 1929 in *Documents*. There, announcing that words should have *jobs* rather than definitions, he says that the job of *formless* is to "déclasser," an action that simultaneously (1) lowers or debases objects by stripping them of their pretensions—in the case of words, their pretensions to meaning—and (2) declassifies, or attacks the very condition on which meaning depends, namely, the structural opposition between definite terms.

With this idea of "declassing," it seemed to me that various strategies in Giacometti's work had found their explanatory model in one go—strategies that ranged from the "lowering" of the normatively vertical axis of free-standing sculpture onto the debased condition of an identity as "mere" sculptural base— the board-game operation, in short—to the "declassifying" or destabilization at large in works like *Suspended Ball,* where formlessness is to be found in a kind of categorical blurring. For in that object, the sexually suggestive sliding of a cloven ball over a recumbent wedge sets up the activity of a caress between organs whose gender identity is wholly unstable, seeming with each swing of the pendulum to change associations: the wedge altering its "state" from a female-labial

Alberto Giacometti, *Suspended Ball,* 1930–31. Plaster and metal, 24 x 14 1/4 x 14 inches. Kunsthaus, Zurich, Alberto Giacometti Foundation. Photo by Walter Drayer.

to a male-phallic condition; the ball transmogrifying to play heterosexual partner to either of those identifications or—buttocks-like—allowing for homoerotic possibilities or, again—suggestive of the eye in either Buñuel and Dali's *Un Chien Andalou* or Bataille's own *Story of the Eye*—setting up the conditions of an ungendered sadism.

The categorical blurring initiated by the continual alteration of identity within this work is precisely what Bataille means by *formless*. It is not just some kind of haze or vagueness in the field of definition, but the impossibility of definition itself due to a strategy of slippage within the very logic of categories, a logic that works according to self-identity—male, say, or female—stabilized by the opposition between self and other: male versus female, hard versus soft, inside versus outside, life versus death, vertical versus horizontal. Nothing indeed could be crisper than the material forms in Giacometti's surrealist sculpture, fashioned first in plaster and then executed by a cabinetmaker in polished wood. The blurring in question, however, is not material but categorical, the work of declassing.

That it can also be called "alteration" is the point of convergence between the general issues of formlessness and the specific analysis of primitivism mounted by Bataille, to which Giacometti seems to have responded. For Bataille was not interested in the formalist appreciation of primitivism so widely celebrated in the 1920s, in which the "primitive" was taken to be synonymous with the creative impulse itself and was consequently seen as giving one access, as it were, to the very birth of form. This birth was pictured as taking place, for example, in the child's first discrimination of closed, repeatable shapes from within the chaos of his or her own scribblings or in the paleolithic painter's similar act of distinction on the walls of the caves or, again, in the genius of the tribal sculptor for finding the primal gestalts through which to figure forth the human body as though in its own process of parturition. Against this connection of the primitive with the creative and the constructive, however, Bataille opposed a primitivism that was violent and destructive, the product of the caves not as the birth of form but as a labyrinthine loss of distinction that is the death of form: art as a function not of Narcissus but of the Minotaur.

Bataille's word for this logic of primitivism was *alteration,* by which he meant both decomposition (as in corpses) and the total otherness of the sacred (as in ghosts). That the word *alteration* could thus, like the Latin *altus,* have the internally contradictory double meaning of both "high" or sacred and "low" or rotten is evidence once more of *formlessness* doing its job. And the alteration Bataille saw at work in the caves, even while the painters promoted the detailed depiction of animal life, was a lowering or debasing of the representation of the specifically *human* form. But striking at the human body in an act of self-mutilation was what Bataille considered the primal fact of marking—not the creation of form but the defacement of it in a gesture that was simultaneously sacred and scatological.

These concepts—formlessness, alteration, and declassing as both lowering and decategorizing—were now available to the project to which I was immediately to turn, namely the analysis of surrealist photography, a phenomenon of surrealist production that was doubly disprivileged within the modernist canon. For if surrealism had been stuck with the accusation that it had added nothing to the repertory of formal innovation in painting and sculpture, photography—marginalized as minor relative to the major art practices—was, in its surrealist guise, derided even within the parameters of its own medium, since photographic values had been declared, from Watkins to Weston, from Atget to Arbus, to be documentary: the previsualization on the camera's ground glass or through its viewfinder of a resulting picture and the brilliant realization of that picture through the vehicle of the print. With this almost hallucinatory transparency by means of which reality—unmanipulated and unretouched—would transport itself into the image, the aesthetics of so-called straight photography were promulgated, an aesthetic based on what Edward Weston termed that "quality of authenticity in the photograph" from which it derives its unimpeachable authority.

The result of this was that all those trick effects with which surrealist practice was identified in the popular imagination—double exposure, sandwich printing, montage, brûlage, solarization—were seen by straight photography as an act of impurity with regard to the medium. As a blurring of the distinction between photograph and painting, or photograph and film, they constituted a

Raoul Ubac, *The Battle of the Amazons (Group III),* 1939. Silver print. Galerie Adrien Maeght, Paris.

Maurice Tabard, *Untitled,* ca. 1930. Silver print. Collection Lucien Treillard, Paris.

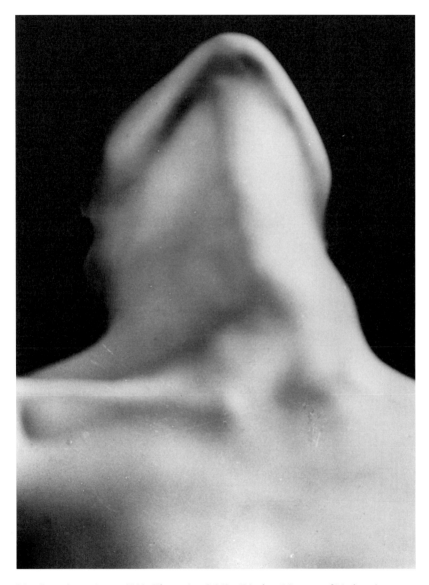

Man Ray, *Anatomies,* ca. 1930. Silver print, 9 1/2 x 7 inches. Museum of Modern Art, New York.

Man Ray, *Hat,* 1933. Silver print, 6 3/4 x 5 1/4 inches. Collection Rosabianca Skira, Geneva.

perverse feminization if you will of the masculinist values of "straightness" itself: clarity, decisiveness, and visual mastery—all of them the source for the photograph's "authority."

Now if *blur* was something my experience with Giacometti had perfectly primed me to find in surrealist photography, it was not the relatively superficial type of blurring that results from the kinds of techniques to which many such practitioners had recourse but just as many did not. Rather it was the deep, categorical blurring involving a transgression of boundaries that I was prepared for and that I found in stunning abundance.

First there was the fall from vertical to horizontal in a cancellation of the distinction between high and low, or between human and animal; then there was the opening of the physical envelope of bodies and objects to a fusion between the inside and the outside of form; or again, there was the enactment of a kind of fetishized vision in which the gender identities of bodies began to slip and the female form (or its proxy) was, for example, reinvested as "phallic." The fact that much of this was performed without darkroom tricks or scissors and paste but rather with a directness that qualified itself as technically "straight" did nothing to remove the categorical blur that had been defiantly branded into the surrealist image and, from the perspective of masculinist photographic values, had "feminized" it.

But then much of what was truly original and far-reaching in surrealist production-across-the-boards was also feminized. The famous passivity with which the surrealists practiced—from Eluard writing mediumistic, or automatic, poetry to Ernst waiting to be struck by the automatist image emerging from the frottage bed—is a kind of feminization of art making, one against which Dali railed as he sought "virility" in the more decisive action available to his paranoid-critical method.

That the passivity to which Dali objected moved from a strategic attitude on the part of the surrealists to a wholly innovative formal principle is the argument Denis Hollier makes with regard to the genre Breton initiated in the autobiographical novels he wrote before the war, beginning with *Nadja,* moving through *Communicating Vessels* and ending in *Mad Love.* Such novels, Hollier says,

Raoul Ubac, *Portrait in a Mirror,* 1938. Silver print, 9 1/2 x 7 inches. Metroplitan Museum of Art, New York.

follow the principle of the diary or for that matter the journalist's report, in which a story is launched without the narrator having the slightest idea of its outcome. Thus if *Nadja* was begun as the account of an episode that had run its course and whose finish Breton knew, the book ends with the unexpected entrance into its pages of a stranger whose arrival could in no way be anticipated at its outset. "The specific feature of Surrealist writing," Hollier urges, "whether it be autobiographical or automatic, is, in fact, less the lack of knowledge of its final destination as such than the identical position into which this lack places both the reader and the author in the face of a text whose unfolding neither the one nor the other controls, and about which both of them know neither the future nor the ending."[5]

The structural passivity that is so important to this conception of writing participates in the conceptual blurring common to the rest of surrealist practice in that it breaks down the difference between those formerly positioned opposites—author and reader—and thus between the inside and the outside of the text. Thus Hollier concludes: "They are, both author and reader, on the same side of the events, on the same side of the page. The one who writes has no privilege, no advance over the one who reads. He doesn't know any more about it than the other."[6]

There are ways in which Hollier's characterization of *Nadja* and Susan Suleiman's presentation of the strategies Marguerite Duras would later employ in her novel *The Ravishing of Lol V. Stein* suggest a strange parallel in this matter of the feminization of the narrator. For in projecting her story of Lol Stein through the halting, hallucinatingly repetitive voice of Jacques Hold, both a participant in the erotic triangle in which he and Lol are caught and the point of view from which that triangulation is seen, Duras has decided to construct a male narrator who is "feminized" and who declares his feminization in terms of his never being able to "know" the object of his gaze: "To have no knowledge at all about Lol," he says, "was to know her already. One could, I realized, know even less, ever less and less, about Lol V. Stein." And this lack of knowledge, which is to say this lack of authority about the giving of both the story's details and its meaning, is intended to function, Suleiman goes on to say, as the thematic

15

mirror for what Duras wants at the level of form—specifically, a type of writing she will also characterize as feminine, a writing that is hesitant, uncertain, full of silences.[7]

It is thus with Duras, a woman writer, that the convergence between two types of marginalization will—in Suleiman's account—be most fully achieved, as the feminine and the avant-garde will each be seen to function as a trope for the other, each a picture of the other's deconstructive strength, won precisely by the position of each outside the self-deceptive and self-blinding occupation of the cultural center with its categorical unities and its assumed truths. In this sense Duras is allowed to epitomize what another feminist critic has seen as being the case for every avant-garde position throughout the twentieth century— namely, "the putting into discourse of 'woman'" or what could be called the avant-garde's "historically unprecedented exploration of the female, differently maternal body."[8]

And yet within Suleiman's own feminist account Duras functions as a double-edged sword. On the one hand in her decision to let her character Jacques Hold tell Lol's story, Duras is a reminder to a certain kind of literalizing stance that a feminist reading that makes every male into an exploiter of women by appropriating both the woman's gaze and her story is a pitifully impoverished reading whose univocal production of its own unwavering point of view amounts to siding, precisely, with the very patriarchy it wishes to contest. But on the other hand, Duras becomes the occasion for Suleiman to deny male *writers* the very possibilities of equivocation to which only she—as a woman author— is seen to have access. For sensitive as she is to the hesitancies and gaps in knowledge of Duras's narrator, Suleiman is unable to see the same qualities projected through Breton's procedures in *Nadja,* which as Hollier has shown are deeply structural to Breton's tale.

To have turned to Susan Suleiman's account of Duras is not a way of abandoning what I named at the outset as the itinerary of my own connection to surrealism, but rather a means of entering more fully into it. For insofar as my position has been centered on the deconstructive logic of surrealism, insofar as I have described surrealist photographers as building a subject position into their work such that its viewer, stripped of authority and dispossessed of privilege, will be "trapped in a cat's cradle of representation, caught in a hall of mirrors, lost in a labyrinth,"[9] I have seen this practice as one of feminizing the viewing subject in a move that is deeply antipatriarchal. Further, insofar as what occurs at the pole of the object is an experience of the gendered subject—most frequently female—as constructed rather than biologically determined, a process of construction the surrealists understood through the terms of psychoanalysis and from which they mined accounts of fetishization and fantasy in order to support a transgressive notion of gender, the surrealists must be seen to have opened patriarchy's view of "woman" up to questioning. It was for this reason that I wrote:

> In much of surrealist practice woman, in being a "shine on the nose" [Freud's first example of the construction of the fetish], is nowhere in nature. Having dissolved the natural in which "normalcy" can be grounded, surrealism was at least potentially open to the dissolving of distinctions that Bataille insisted was the job of the *informe*. Gender, at the heart of the surrealist project was one of these categories. If within surrealist poetry /woman/ was constantly in construction, then at certain moments that project could at least prefigure a next step in which a reading is opened onto deconstruction.[10]

And accordingly, I concluded, a view of surrealism as simply misogynist or antifeminist is mistaken.

The indignant dismissals of this position on the part of feminist writers who have accused me of a "collusion with the male gaze" that has blinded me to the surrealists' deep misogyny have mostly been of the type that Suleiman found herself fending off in the case of Duras's use of Jacques Hold as the narrator of Lol Stein's story.[11] But Suleiman has also found herself worrying about my account of the movement; for, given the fact that the surrealist photographers presented there are consistently male, she wonders whether its "figural substitution of 'woman' or 'the feminine' for avant-garde practice [ends up by] eliding precisely the question of the female subject."[12] Indeed, she goes on to ask

17

"whether the 'putting into discourse of "woman"' by a woman writer is comparable, in its meaning and effects, to its putting into discourse by a male writer" and, maintaining that it is not, she concludes that "a woman Surrealist cannot simply assume a subject position and take over a stock of images elaborated by the male imaginary." In order to innovate, Suleiman maintains:

> she has to invent her own position as subject and elaborate her own set of images—different from the image of the exposed female body, yet as empowering as that image is, with its endless potential for manipulation, disarticulation and rearticulation, fantasizing and projection, for her male colleagues.[13]

Concluding that there *were* such women within the movement and that henceforth it will be irresponsible for anyone speaking of surrealism not to devote considerable attention to them, she admits, after listing such figures as Leonora Carrington, Dorothea Tanning, Kay Sage, Leonor Fini, Valentine Hugo, and Unica Zürn, that these were practitioners who entered the movement only after it started its decline and, further, ones whose practice is most adequately described through the notion of "mimicry" in which the "woman 'repeats' the male—in this case, the male Surrealist—version of 'woman,' but does so in a self-conscious way that points up the citational, often ironic status of the repetition."[14]

The idea of the gender specificity of the authorial subject, or rather the certainty that gender necessarily divides the population of authors such that the only way female artists could share a vision with male ones would be either through collusion with a male gaze or by means of an ironizing, distancing resort to "mimicry"—in which imitation is self-consciously performed as apotropaic gesture—is something I wish to contest as introduction to a book on the work of women artists. For in the matter of surrealism, and more specifically in the case of its photographic practice, I think that some of the most emblematic work of the movement—most emblematic in the sense of both most representative and most powerful—was done by women.

A particular case I have in mind is a pair of photomontages by Dora Maar, works that have the same amazing economy as anything one can think of by Brassaï—the nudes he made for the inaugural issue of *Minotaure* (1933), for instance—or by Man Ray—his *Minotaure* (1934), for example, or his *Anatomies* (1930), or his hat-as-fetish (1933). In all of these the categorical blurring in an otherwise perfectly focused image produces a slippage in gender that ends by figuring forth that image of the body-in-alternation that is projected by the phallic woman. In Dora Maar's examples the phallic character of the legs—their distension and rigidity—needs no underlining, nor perhaps does the registration of lack that will supply the signifier of the feminine component of this ambivalent sign. In one case this is marked by a gap between the two legs articulated by a rivulet of hair; in the other it is performed as a flange of drapery, or women's underpants as the metonymy of a cleft.

But something else grips these images and allies them with other works equally central to the movement; and that is the registration through them of the presence of the praying mantis, an insect epitomized by being almost nothing but a pair of stalklike legs and notorious for fusing sex with death since the female of the species is known to cannibalize her male partner directly after mating. The parallel such a recognition provokes is with whole ranges of Bellmer's *Poupées,* not simply because of their own drive to construct the feminine body as tumescent or erectile, but more particularly to cast it, mantislike, as nothing but legs and in that guise as profoundly threatening: the very image of the Medusa in all its castrative menace.

I introduce this parallel not only to show how fully Dora Maar is participating in various visual and psychological tropes employed by her male colleagues—and I can see not the slightest evidence that such participation is in any way ironic—but also to challenge the interpretative reflex that would label this kind of work—with its invocation of the mantis, the Medusa, and the whole freight of castration anxiety they carry—as misogynist. The attack on the male ego—on its wholeness, its strength, and its stable center—is the task of the Medusa who, acting against the armoring of the male psyche, works to shatter it. An alliance with the Medusa is thus not an attack on women, but an assault on a viewer assumed to be male and an award to his fantasies of their worst fears.

———

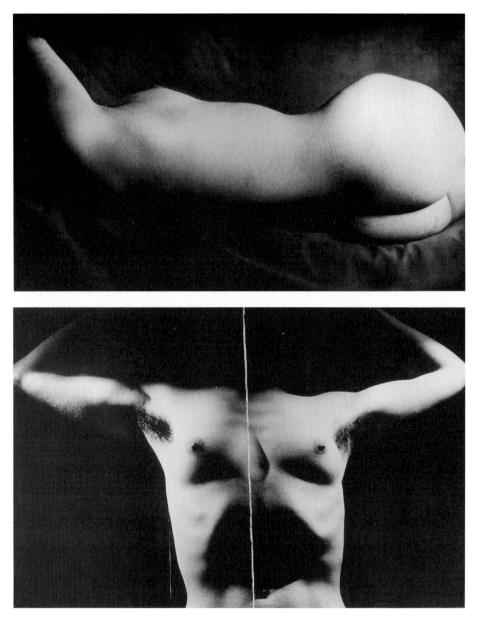

Brassai, *Nude,* 1933. Silver print. Collection Rosabianca Skira, Geneva.

Man Ray, *Minotaure,* 1933. Silver print. Private collection, Paris.

———

Hans Bellmer, *La Poupée,* 1936/1949. Tinted silver print, 16 1/8 x 13 inches. Musée National d'Art Modern, Paris.

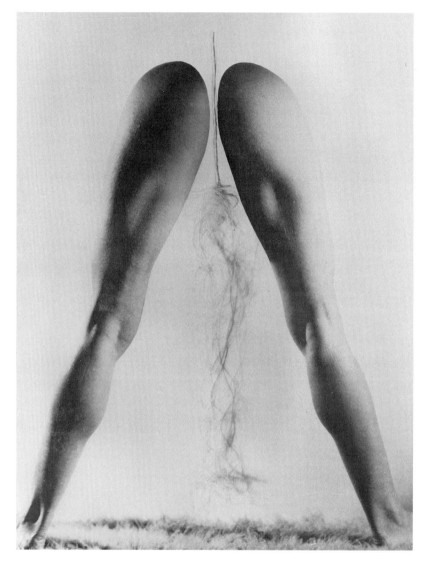

Dora Maar, *Untitled,* ca. 1936. Silver print.

Dora Maar, *Untitled,* ca. 1936. Silver print.

This is the argument that Hal Foster makes in relation to Bellmer's *Poupées:* namely that they assault the Nazi subject with the very menace that subject fears, which is not attack by a figure of power but invasion by a group of others who, although identified as weak, nonetheless threaten its borders both geographically (Jews, homosexuals, gypsies, Bolsheviks) and psychically (the unconscious, sexuality, the "feminine"). This fear of invasion, pathological in the fascist subject, must in its turn be seen as the projection of a fantasized bodily chaos against which that subject armors himself, seeking a defense by means of a metallicized human body whose aesthetic expression is a hardened and vulgarized neoclassicism. If Bellmer's project submits itself to sadomasochistic fantasies in order to explore the tension between the binding and shattering of the ego, this, Foster argues, is to assume a complicity with the fascist subject "only to expose it most effectively," since in the *Poupées,* he says, "this fear of the destructive and the diffusive is made manifest and reflexive, as is the attempt to overcome it in violence against the feminine other—that is a scandal but also a lesson of the dolls."[15]

That it is the Nazi subject that Bellmer is targeting is made particularly explicit in one of the dolls in which the wheel of bent legs rotating around a central ball joint is made to take the configuration of a swastika. The swastikoid Medusa is not only a shattering image for the armored male ego but one that has picked out its receiver.

In Dora Maar's photograph to which she gave the name *Père Ubu,* her identification of the formlessness of the weakened boundary is represented more famously if not more powerfully than in her two pairs of legs. Shown in 1936 at the Charles Ratton Gallery where it presided over the surrealist objects exhibition, Dora Maar's *Ubu* functioned from the very start, in fact, as the emblematic surrealist photograph, having gone on to become a kind of mascot of the movement.

It is not Dora Maar, however, but Claude Cahun who has recently emerged as a powerful answer to Suleiman's call for a woman surrealist who would "invent her own position as subject and elaborate her own set of images— different from the image of the exposed female body, yet as empowering as that

Hans Bellmer, *La Poupée,* 1938. Tinted silver print, 11 x 19 1/4 inches. Private collection, Paris.

Hans Bellmer, *La Poupée (Idole),* 1937. Tinted silver print, 5 1/2 x 5 1/2 inches. Private collection, Paris.

Hans Bellmer, *La Poupée,* 1938. Tinted silver print, 5 1/2 x 5 1/2 inches. Private collection, Paris.

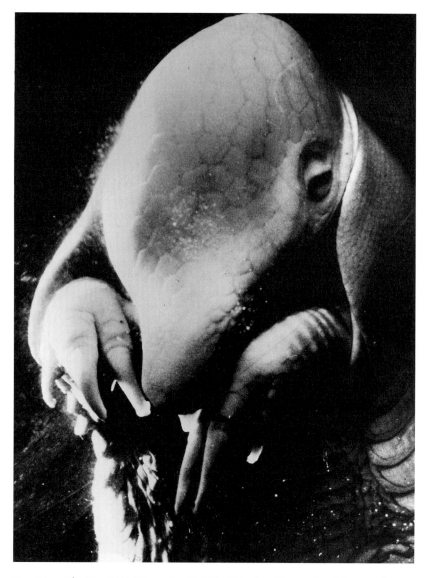

Dora Maar, *Père Ubu,* 1936. Silver print, 15 1/2 x 11 inches. Metropolitan Museum of Art, New York.

image is . . . for her male colleagues." I say recently emerged because Cahun was so little known from the time of her death until the past decade that reviewers of the exhibition that included her, *L'Amour Fou: Surrealism and Photography*— even reviewers well versed in surrealism—assumed that with a first name like Claude, she had to be male. And this oblivion was further marked by the fact that important anthologies devoted to the movement's women, such as the 1976 special issue of *Obliques* called "La Femme Surréaliste," or *Surrealism and Women* edited by Mary Anne Caws, Rudolf Kuenzli, and Gwen Raaberg, or Whitney Chadwick's *Women Artists and the Surrealist Movement* (1985), never mention Cahun.

But Cahun—surrealist writer, photographer, actress, political activist, participant in the French resistance, and flamboyant lesbian—has come to stand for an engagement with the construction of both identity and gender, as well an exploration of the labile condition of subjectivity, which many feminist writers find exemplary.[16] It is to this end that these critics inevitably turn to Cahun's various statements about her assumption of the condition of masquerade, citing with approval, for instance, the lines from her autobiographical *Canceled Confessions* in which she states: "Under this mask, another mask. I will never finish removing all these faces."

Indeed Cahun's entry into the world of the Parisian literary avant-garde was marked by her adopting a pseudonym, the first name of which—Claude— announced a gender indeterminacy that further adjustments in her physical appearance and self-presentation would reinforce. Shaving her head, or dying the short crew cut she sometimes allowed to grow pink or green, she adopted a mask of masculinity that she further exaggerated, for example, in the photographic self-portraits that distort her skull through anamorphosis, or in the male parts she chose to play in Albert-Birot's theater. But when she decided to appear as feminine, this too was projected as constantly mediated either through the mask of makeup and artifice or through the series of actual masks she assumed and with which she surrounded herself. These remarkable self-portraits, which serve as a series of baffles behind which the "real" Claude Cahun disappears, function further as the material from which Moore, Cahun's half-sister and lover, created

---

Claude Cahun, *Self-Portrait,* ca. 1928. Silver print. San Francisco Museum of Modern Art, Gift of Robert Shapazian.

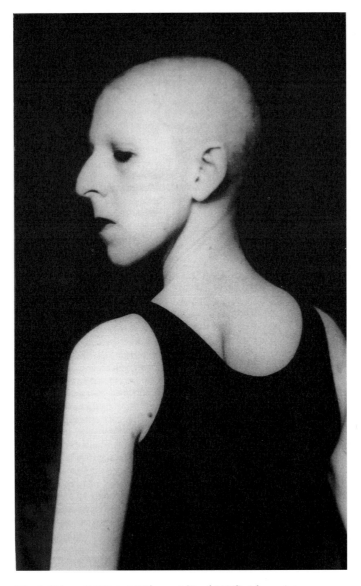

Claude Cahun, *Self-Portrait* (*Bifur* no. 5 [April 1930]). Silver print.

Claude Cahun, *Self-Portrait,* ca. 1921. Zabriskie Gallery, New York.

Claude Cahun, *Self-Portrait,* 1929. Silver print. San Francisco Museum of Modern Art, Gift of Robert Shapazian.

Claude Cahun, *Self-Portrait,* ca. 1928. Silver print. Private collection, Paris.

Claude Cahun, *Self-Portrait,* ca. 1928. Silver print. Boymans Museum, Rotterdam.

Claude Cahun, *Self-Portrait,* ca. 1927. Silver print. Berggruen Gallery, Paris.

photomontages to mark the ten sections of *Aveux non avenues* (or *Canceled Confessions*), Cahun's collection of autobiographical narratives, poems, accounts of dreams, and reflections on the condition of identity.

Insofar as these reflections challenge the very idea of selfhood as stable, as in her formula "'To mirror' and 'to stabilize'—these are words that have no business here," Cahun's deconstructive stance on the position of the subject is continuous with the subjective *blurring* I have been attributing to much of surrealist production and discussing under the concepts "formless," "alteration," or "declassing." And indeed, insofar as many of Cahun's visual tropes pressed into the creation of her masks use the same props to produce the same effects of disarticulation and rearticulation, or of fantasizing and projection, as were employed by her male colleagues, there is a further continuity between her work and theirs. I am thinking specifically, here, of her placing her head under a bell jar in a way that resembles the photograph Man Ray would call *Homage to D.A.F. de Sade,* or her use of fun-fair mirrors to attack her own anatomy as in Kertesz's *Distortions,* or her decision to curl up in a cupboard and assume the limpness and docility of a doll as in Bellmer's *Poupées.*

But to the very idea that Cahun's exploration of boundary conditions might resemble that of the male surrealists, her feminist supporters object that Cahun's autobiographical project not only puts her on both sides of the camera—simultaneously the subject and object of representation—but it also endows her, a woman, with the power of both projecting the gaze and returning it, as Claude's eyes meet ours, sometimes seductively, sometimes hostilely, sometimes quizzically, from within the image. Indeed, they go on to say, the very enterprise of self-portraiture, otherwise so absent from the entire corpus of surrealist photography, comes down to reclaiming agency for the female subject.

In all the discussions of Cahun's change of name as the expression of transvestitism and thus as emblematic of her decision to suspend the fixity of gender, there is almost no comment on the part of her pseudonym that does not bear on matters of sex but rather on questions of race. Indeed, the subject who was born Lucy Schwob, into an extremely prominent literary family, initially embraced the pen name Claude Courlis to publish a text in 1914 in *Le Mercure de France,*

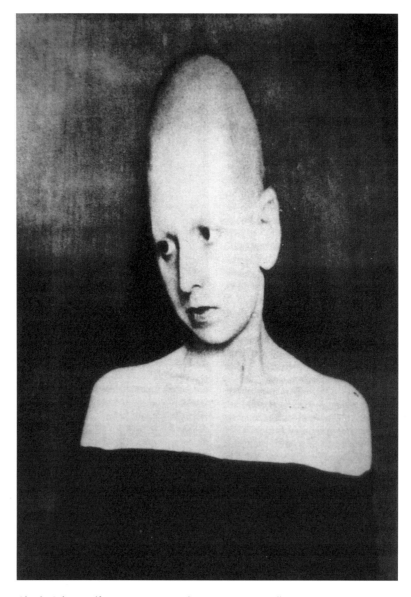

Claude Cahun, *Self-Portrait,* ca. 1929. Silver print. Private collection, Paris.

André Ketesz, *Distortion #6,* 1932. Silver print, 9 3/16 x 7 3/16 inches. Metropolitan Museum of Art, New York.

Hans Bellmer, *La Poupée,* 1935. Silver print. Collection, François Petit, Paris.

Claude Cahun, *Self-Portrait,* ca. 1932. Silver print. John Wakeham Collection, New Jersey.

the journal her famous uncle, Marcel Schwob, had helped found. But this embrace of masculinity was followed by yet a second problematizing of identity when, in 1918, for another text in the same journal she assumed the last name Cahun. Undoubtedly significant that she was thereby assuming the name of her mother's family, what has consistently gone without comment is that Cahun is a French form of Cohen, and thus identifies its bearer as belonging to the rabbinical class among Jews, just as Levy would identify *its* bearer as belonging to the subpriestly liturgical class. Though undeniably Jewish, the name Schwob had assumed a certain cultural veneer that armed its bearer somewhat against anti-Semitism, joining it to "Proust," among others. The act of defiance attached to leaving "Schwob" to affect "Cahun" can thus only be seen as one of flaunting one's Jewishness in the face of the heightened anti-Semitism of postwar France, a kind of provocation every bit as dangerous as parading one's lesbianism.

Now Claude Cahun was not the only member of the postwar avant-garde in France to couple *travestie* and Jewishness in one defiant gesture. Marcel Duchamp tells Pierre Cabanne that when he wanted to change his identity in 1920, the first idea that came to him was to take a Jewish name. Saying "I didn't find a Jewish name that I especially liked, or that tempted me, and suddenly I had an idea: why not change sex? . . . the name Rrose Sélavy came from that,"[17] Duchamp simply slides by the fact that his final choice allowed him to "change sex" and "take a Jewish name" at one and the same time, since Levy—the second most Jewish name, after Cohen—is unmistakably folded into Sélavy.

This parallel between Cahun and Duchamp, alias Rrose Sélavy, clearly goes past the fact of the names, moving into the whole project of self-portraiture that both of them shared, a project not only explored through photography but also in the written and other forms of their work. And insofar as both of them mark this exploration by means of a fold in the field of representation, a fold around which not only identities revolve and reflect like a pair of double helixes but also the positions of viewer and viewed become reversible, the parallel becomes all the more compelling.

The fold in Cahun's work results not only from her use of a mirror to produce the effect of the real as a kind of giant Rorschach blot, in which

Claude Cahun, *Self-Portrait,* ca. 1919. Silver print. Zabriskie Gallery, New York.

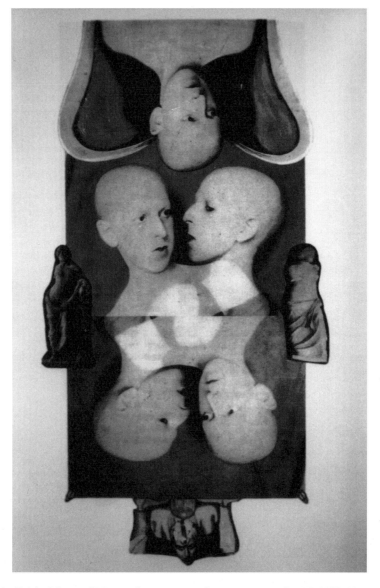

Claude Cahun and Moore, photomontage, *Aveux non avenus,* plate IV, 1929–30.

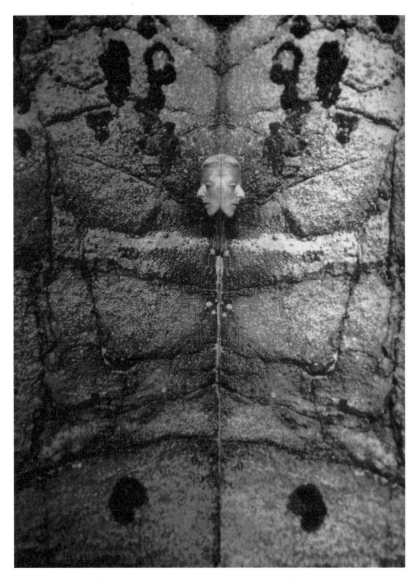

Claude Cahun, *Self-Portrait,* photomontage, ca. 1928. Private collection, Paris.

Marcel Duchamp, note from *The Green Box,* reproduced in Michel Sanouillet and Elmer Peterson, eds., *Salt Seller: The Writings of Marcel Duchamp (Marchand du Sel)* (New York: Oxford University Press, 1973), 39.

authentic and copy chase each other's tail, but also of course from her use of masks to create a kind of fold in the realm of subjectivity—personhood exfoliating into persona. Such a fold is plotted at many points in Duchamp's exploration of identity, beginning with the horizon line of the *Large Glass* that separates the realm of the Bachelors from that of the Bride, a line Duchamp would express as a fold in his own subjectivity in the little sketch he made for the notes for the *Glass* where the realm above the fold is given as MAR (for Mariée) and the one below it as CEL (for Célibataires) so that, run together, they produce a "Marcel" bisected through gender.

But Duchamp is also at pains to make clear that the fold is the nexus as well of a kind of directional reversibility, as in the action of the Rotoreliefs, Rrose Sélavy's own artistic product. There, projected through the 1923 *Anémic Cinéma,* the turning discs initiate a movement that soon creates the illusion that it has reversed itself: protruding eye or breast, for example, becoming the retreating hollow of uterine cavity; or, in the field of language, the left-right reversal of the *contrepetrie,* or spoonerism, folding the word *esquimaux,* for example, back on itself to become *aux mots exquis.* Further, this doubling of a fold in identity with a spatial fold that reverses directions so that viewer might change places with viewed, or addressor with addressee, is expressed in the strange self-portrait Duchamp called *Tu m'* where the poles "you" and "me" are suggested as being reversible much as in the psychological phenomenon of transitivism, in which, for instance, a child who sees another being slapped begins to cry, believing itself to be the recipient of the blow.[18]

That the surrealists would have embraced this practice of the fold, so that in the field of language Robert Desnos would have published poetry consisting of spoonerisms and signed Rose Sélavy, or Michel Leiris would publish the same form under the title "Glossaire: Je serre mes glosses," is significant in the particular way it inscribes Duchamp within the field of the surrealism of the mid-1920s. But in the matter of a parallel use of the folded self-portrait to explore identity, Duchamp and Cahun should be placed in explicit relationship, I would argue, to allow us to feel the extent to which such a fold disrupts the fixed positions of the viewer as much as that of the viewed. If we recognize that through the work,

Marcel Duchamp, *Disc with Inscriptions of Calembours: "Des Esquimaux,"* 30 cm. diameter, 1926.

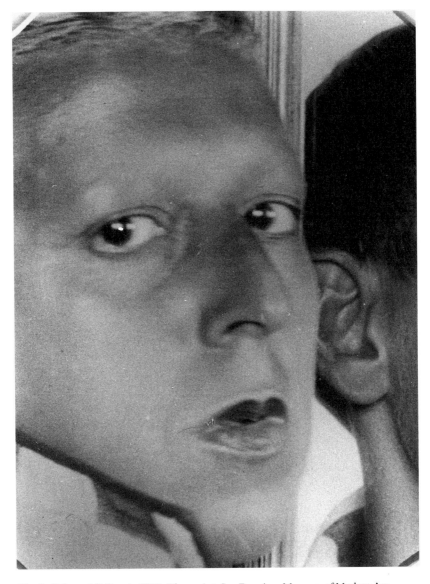

Claude Cahun, *Self-Portrait,* 1928. Silver print. San Francisco Museum of Modern Art, Gift of Robert Shapazian.

on either side of the line that divides subject and object, male and female identi-fications are continuously changing places, it is not possible to take such a project seriously and at one and the same time to proclaim the subject-position of the work's instigator as stable and female, as has been urged for Cahun.

Another way to put this would be to ask whether there is a material difference between her treatment of the field of representation and that of Du-champ or between her use of masquerade and his—beyond the fact that as a younger artist and a surrealist, her work projects a sense of psychological inten-sity and disturbance that his avoids.

I do not ask this question to depreciate Cahun's work but rather to distance myself from the assumption that resonates from within Suleiman's (but I am only citing her as the strongest such example) invocation of something called "the male imaginary." For the parallel between Cahun and Duchamp is meant to ar-gue for a fluidity in the field of the Imaginary that allows for its positions to be occupied by more than one gender at once. To say this is to assert that art made by women needs no special pleading, and in the essays that follow I will offer none.

Louise Bourgeois: Portrait of the Artist as *Fillette*

Her portrait by Robert Mapplethorpe, taken in 1982, shows her grinning imp-ishly at the camera, swathed in a coat of dark, shaggy wool, jauntily carrying one of her sculptures under her arm as though it were an umbrella or a cane that her cupped hand supports at the object's protruding, forward end. But the sculpture is not an umbrella or a cane. Called *Fillette* and dated 1968, it resembles nothing so much as an outsized dildo, an association heightened by the way the photo-graph profiles the twin ball-like forms that make up the sculpture's nether region, and at the other end, highlights its rigid shaft and rounded, furrowed tip. Is Lou-ise Bourgeois's grin, which breaks her face into a luminously soft series of eddies and ripples, the response to her own imagining of the provocativeness of this image?

Nearly ten years before, another woman artist, from an entirely different generation, had had herself photographed, a dildo held erect from between the legs of her naked body. Lynda Benglis's paid advertisement, published in *Artforum* in November 1974, proclaimed the message of many young artists coming into their own in the 1970s. The art world, it seemed to say, is being restructured as a star system in which the artist is increasingly a commodity, a personality to be packaged and sold. Warhol had said it all, the ad proclaimed, and hucksterism had replaced aesthetics. Here is my body. Buy me.

Robert Mapplethorpe, *Portrait of Louise Bourgeois,* 1982.

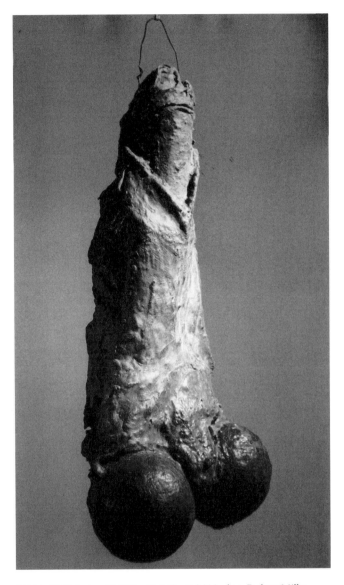

Fillette, 1968. Latex, 23 3/8 x 10 1/2 x 7 3/4 inches. Robert Miller
Gallery, New York.

But Louise Bourgeois is an artist of the immediate postwar period—of the late 1940s and the 1950s—not of the generation of the seventies. So her portrait, of the artist clutching *Fillette,* locates itself in relation to quite another set of issues. It has more to do with Brancusi's *Princess X,* than with Lynda Benglis's advertisement for herself. Its "scandal" is more firmly placed within the territory of the sculptural and less within the world of the social. For the scandal of *Princess X,* one that caused it to be peremptorily removed from the 1920 Salon des Indépendants, was that the sculpture looked unmistakably, graphically, phallic.

Art historians have thought this reaction against the public display of the phallic object not so much prudish as misguided. The "partial figure"—as they call the various modernist truncations of the body, into torso, hand, thigh, breast, penis, as in Rodin, Maillol, Brancusi . . . —is a formal matter, a declaration against the narrative of gesture, for example, or the inescapable realism of the body whole. It is about the purification and reduction of form. If partial figures had, in the past, been limited to what one historian calls "a special case in sculpture, comprising the portrait bust, religious symbolism such as ancient phallic-cult images, and decorative art where it took the form of the caryatid," modernist logic seemed to have generalized this special case into the very formal conditions of sculpture itself.[1] Promoted particularly by the study of classical remains in the form of antique fragments, nineteenth-century romantic enthusiasm for the fragment, the historians argue, turned into twentieth-century conviction that it was the vehicle for a profound, sculptural truth. The body contracted into its most powerful synecdoches: the body as egg, the body as tree trunk, the body as spoonlike hollow. And egg, tree trunk, spoon are themselves moving in the direction of abstraction, they add. The body as perfect sphere, the body as cylinder, the body as simple, concave plane.

But another reading of the history of much of modernist sculpture is that it locates itself not so much in the domain of the "partial figure" as of the part-object, the part-object given its psychoanalytic dimension as the goal of an instinct or drive. The body of the subject, focused around so many separate organs and their needs and desires, interacts with the world outside itself—the object-world—in terms of the reciprocal organs that will satisfy those needs and desires:

the world of the infant as so many breasts, mouths, bellies, penises, anuses. . . . The part-object speaks to the imperiousness of the drives, to the rapacity of their demands, to the way the body can, in the grip of fantasy, be riven, cannibalized, shattered.

There is nothing "abstract" about the part-object. But its logic, which spells the connection between agents—the desiring organs on the one hand and the yielding or withholding objects of desire on the other—rather than between individuals or "whole" persons, is reductive: the mother reduced to breast.

The extraordinary thing about the reception of Louise Bourgeois's sculpture from its first appearance at the end of the 1940s up to the late 1980s is that it was consistently described as abstract, abstract in the sense of a modernist formal logic. There was almost always an admission that the aura of the human body clings to the work, that there are erotic connotations, that the sexual organs are somehow figured forth within it, that there are associations made to tribal art. But nowhere in the literature on this sculpture was there a mention of the part-object, even though this is work in which breasts (*Trani Episode* [1971–72]), penises (*Pregnant Woman* [1947–49], *Janus in Leather Jacket* [1968]), clitorises (*Femme Couteau* [1969–70]), vaginas (*Janus Fleuri* [1968]), (*Torso/Self-Portrait* [1965–66]), uteruses (*Le Regard,* [1966]) confront us singly (*Fillette*) or in groups (*Double Negative* [1963]), and in which the choice of sculptural medium—rubber latex, plastic, plaster, wax, resin, hemp—is consistently pushed toward the evocation of bodily organs and even the treatment of traditional materials like marble and bronze succeeds in capturing the tautness of swollen flesh, the shininess of membranous tissue. Nowhere, that is to say, was the expectation of an encounter with abstract sculpture made to admit that it is face to face with the reality of organs.

But then this is also true of the literature on Brancusi, which is particularly fond of describing the work in terms of geometric purity, idealized Platonic solids, reductions away from the human and into an ideated sphere. And what this misses is what we could call the organ-logic of Brancusi's work, its dynamic. The gleaming polished bronze egglike form of *The Newborn* (1920) collapses onto one and the same volume the infant's demanding mouth and the mother's

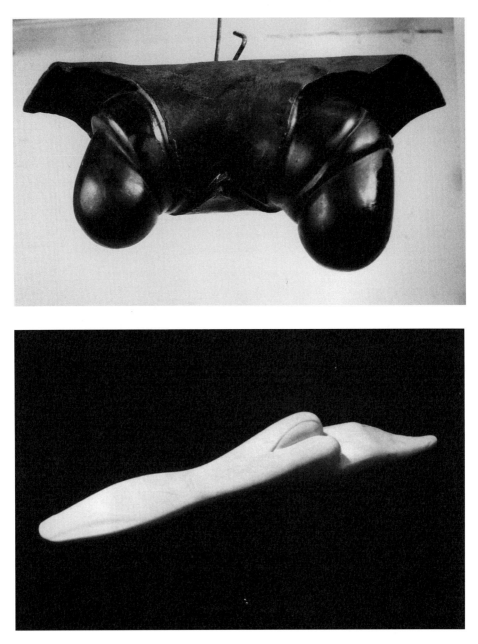

Janus in Leather Jacket, 1968. Bronze, 12 x 22 x 6 1/2 inches. Robert Miller Gallery, New York.

Femme Couteau, 1969. Pink marble, 3 1/2 x 26 3/8 x 4 7/8 inches. Jerry and Emily Spiegel Collection, New York.

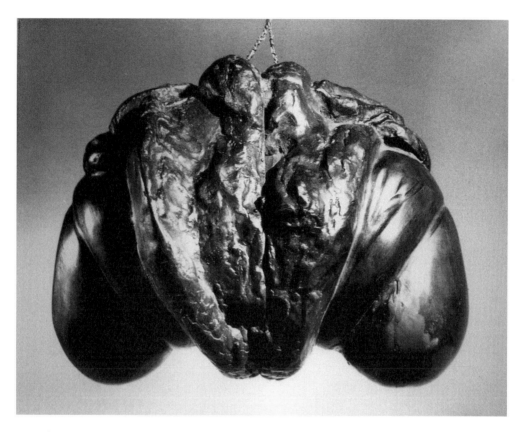

Janus Fleuri, 1968. Bronze, 10 1/8 x 12 1/2 x 8 3/8 inches. Galerie Lelong, Zurich.

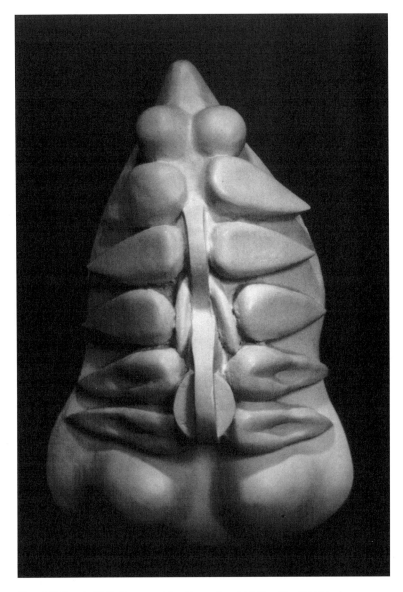

Torso Self-Portrait, 1969. Bronze with white patina, 24 3/4 x 16 x 7 1/2 inches.
Robert Miller Gallery, New York.

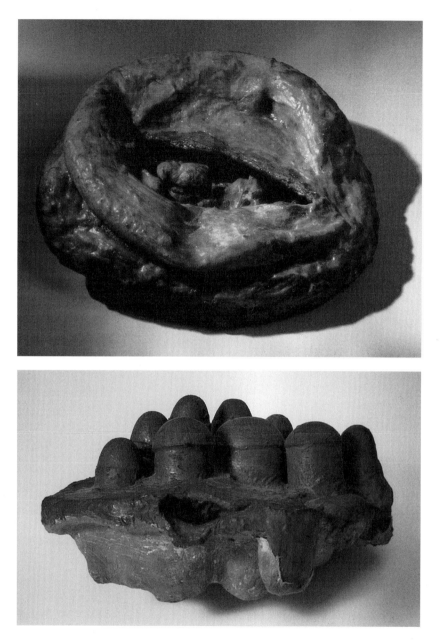

Le Regard, 1966. Latex and fabric, 5 x 15 1/2 x 14 1/2 inches. Robert Miller Gallery, New York.

Double Negative, 1963. Plaster and latex, 19 3/8 x 37 1/2 x 70 1/2 inches. Galerie Lelong, Zurich.

———

yielding breast, while its very mirrorlike surface, reflecting everything in the surrounding space onto its own exterior skin, underscores this logic of fusion between part-objects, a logic that Melanie Klein was to call introjection/projection. Or again, *Torso of a Young Man* (1916), resembling the inverted crotch of tree trunk and branches, projects the smooth "castrated" torso of the mother as itself redoubled as the erect penis of the desiring child. In the space of desire, the space of the part-object and its logic, organs attach to one another and fuse with one another through the fantasy of introjection.

*

The series of paintings and drawings Bourgeois made in the late 1940s, many of them called *Femme-Maison,* some of them abstract configurations of hatched lines, are instantly reminiscent of a variety of surrealist art. Generally speaking, the organization of the *Femme-Maison* works, with their layering into three or four vertically stacked segments that brings about a sense of abrupt stylistic discontinuity between the house form and that of the lower part of the woman to which the house abuts, promotes a strong sense of the surrealist *exquisite corpse*—a form of collective drawing that produces conglomerate figures. More specifically, in the manner of setting up the strangely empty space, and in the primitiveness of the drawing, as well as in the theme of human figure collapsed with objects or architecture, one feels a relationship to the work of Victor Brauner, Toyen, and perhaps Mimi Parent. But behind the styles of these latter three artists there is another element in turn, one that affected all of surrealism of the late 1930s and 1940s; this is the experience, vigorously promoted by André Breton, of art made by schizophrenics. The concatenated images and rigid outlines of now-famous mental patients such as Aloyse, Klotz, Wölffli, and Neter, all had their effect on surrealist production. The most notorious case of this is the composite image Max Ernst called *Oedipus* and published in *Le Surréalisme au Service de la Révolution* (no. 5, 1933), a work that seems to have been inspired by Neter's extraordinary drawing called *Miraculous Shepherd.* And in Louise Bourgeois's works of this time Neter is certainly present also, as is a kind of obsessional doodling style, made famous in André Breton's essay "Le Message

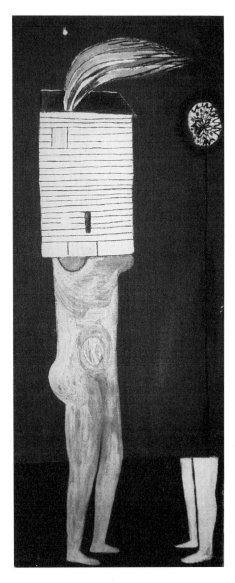

Femme Maison, 1945–47. Oil and ink on linen,
36 x 14 inches. Agnes Gund Collection.

Automatique,"[2] in which a kind of electrically charged nonfigurative topography is wrought by parallel hatched lines.

Is it really still necessary to state that to speak of these connections—Bourgeois/Brauner/Toyen/schizophrenic art—is not to place any one artist in the series in a slavish relation to any other? Is it necessary to insist that resemblances such as these are far more general than anything that art history likes to refer to as "influence"? Rather, from the time it had entered the consciousness of artists and writers in the early 1920s (introduced by Hans Prinzhorn's influential book, *The Art of the Insane* [1922]), schizophrenic art had an extremely strong grip on cultural imagination. It was formative of the thinking not only of artists like Ernst and Masson, and writers like Artaud, but intellectuals like Roger Caillois, and psychoanalysts like Jacques Lacan, whose first published work examined schizophrenic writing.

If it is interesting to note that Bourgeois's presculptural work participates in this general exploration of the features of schizophrenic art, it is only because the structure of that art can be seen to connect, ultimately, to the experience of the part-object. For the most dramatic cases of subjects entirely trapped within the logic of the part-object are those now-famous accounts of schizophrenic children.

Melanie Klein tells the story of the little affectless boy called Dick. She recounts his first visit to her office:

> When I showed him the toys I had put ready, he looked at them without the faintest interest. I took a big train and put it beside a smaller one and called them "Daddy-train" and "Dick-train." Thereupon he picked up the train I called "Dick" and made it roll to the window and said "Station." I explained: "The station is mummy; Dick is going into mummy." He left the train, ran into the space between the outer and inner doors of the room, shutting himself in, saying "dark," and ran out again directly. He went through this performance several times. I explained to him: "It is dark inside mummy. Dick is inside dark mummy." Meantime he picked up the

train again, but soon ran back into the space between the doors. While I was saying that he was going into dark mummy, he said twice in a questioning way: "Nurse?" . . . As his analysis progressed Dick had also discovered the wash-basin as symbolizing the mother's body, and he displayed an extraordinary dread of being wetted with water."[3]

The experience of the self as a set of objects and the need to connect each object to a network of other objects finds another dramatic example in the autistic child Joey, described by Bruno Bettelheim.[4] Joey, who understands himself to be a machine—a sequence of gears and buttons and circuitry—believes that all of his life functions will only work if he, a machine, is plugged into other machines that will, with their motors whirring and their lights blinking, allow him to breathe, to eat, to defecate. "Connecticut," Joey cries. "Connect-I-cut."

*

The logic of "Connect-I-cut" and the logic of the part-object engage Gilles Deleuze and Félix Guattari in their essay on "Desiring Machines," the chapter that opens *Anti-Oedipus,* their study of schizo-captialism. Beginning by saying that "a schizophrenic out for a walk is a better model than a neurotic lying on the analyst's couch," Deleuze and Guattari point to the self-descriptions of famous schizophrenics—one is Judge Schreber, another Atonin Artaud, yet another is Beckett's fictional character Molloy—all of whom convey the dismembering logic of the part-object.[5] Gone is the experience of the whole body, of the integrated individual. Instead there are organs—breasts, anuses, mouths, penises—each with its own imperious demands. And these, the part-objects, each seeking another part-object onto which to attach, Deleuze and Guattari call the desiring machines. The attachment is Joey's "connect"—the plug-in logic of the machine. But the "I-cut" refers to the work of the machine, the product of which is to resegment reality, to slice the continuous flows of energy that surge through it into sections. The desiring machines produce by intercepting the continuous flows of milk, urine, semen, fecal matter; they interrupt one flow in order to produce another, which the next machine will interrupt to produce a flow for the next, and so on. Each machine is a part-object: the breast-machine, the mouth-machine, the stomach-machine, the intestine-machine, the anus-machine. And the connections forged between these machines is a function of the fact that each machine produces the flow that the next machine wants. For Deleuze and Guattari this logic of machines, flows, connections, and production is important. For it displaces fantasy and desire from its traditional, psychoanalytically understood realm of ideality—something that happens in the head (in the unconscious, in dreams, etc.)—and moves it into the material domain. It becomes something that takes place in the field of the real.

The part-object is, then, translated by Deleuze and Guattari into the desiring machine in order to insist on the reality of the machine's production, and to counteract the Kleinian, and Freudian, tendency to speak of its activity as symbolic only. The interest taken by the authors of *Anti-Oedipus* in the "model" of schizophrenia stems from the degree to which the schizophrenic actually reworks reality to conform to this logic. But they are equally interested in the model provided by another tradition of production, one which arose early in this century and to which has been given another name, that of "bachelor machine."

In 1952 Michel Carrouges published a study of this phenomenon, the shared creation of a series of distinguished twentieth-century writers and artists. Comparing Franz Kafka's mechanism for torture through tattooing in *The Penal Colony,* Villier de l'Isle Adam's infinitely seductive female robot in *L'Eve future,* and Raymond Roussel's machines for textual production in *Impressions of Africa,* Carrouges began to perceive an imaginative pattern, one that he called the "bachelor machine" after its most complete example: Marcel Duchamp's *La mariée mise à nu par ses célibataires, même.* Robotic, the bachelor machines involve a perpetual motion that takes them outside the field of organic procreation. Beyond the cycle of fecundation/birth/life/death, they constitute a dream of both infinite celibacy and total autoeroticism. Their life, which is in fact a continual death, is the production of a kind of continual absence, for what they produce is writing, or text. This is true of Kafka's tattoos, of Roussel's painting or weaving machines, of the recordings built by Edison into the Eve imagined by Villier. Duchamp's *Large Glass* is, of course, the most specific model of the machine, its most perfected instance. Everything is there: the plan for perpetual motion that the "Litanies" chant as "vicious circle"; the complexity of the interconnections—glider, malic molds, sieves, chocolate grinder, scissors. . . ; the sterility of the cycle, its autoeroticism, its narcissism; the utter self-enclosure of the system, in which desire is at one and the same time producer, consumer, and re-producer (recorder or copier)—which is to say, the bachelor apparatus below, the occulist witnesses in mirrored disks on the right, the top inscription of the bride above, in the cloud Duchamp identified as "the blossoming."

The world constructed by Kafka or Villier or Roussel is fictional, but within that world the bachelor machine acts in "reality," not in fantasy. Likewise, Duchamp suspends his laboriously "realistic" bachelor apparatus in a field of glass to give it the utmost illusion of actually being in the real space of its installation. The insertion of desire in the space of the real, and the insistence on the reality of its production, is the effort of the works presented by Carrouges, as it was to become the effort of Breton as he theorized the position of surrealism. All of this is, then, "anti-Oedipal" in the Deleuzian sense. All of it wants to counter the idea of art as symbolic, as hidden away in the world of fantasy, as placed on the shelves of a library or the pedestals of a museum. Desire, they insist, acts in the field of the real; it produces.

Not surprisingly, sculpture finds itself right in the middle of a battle about whether it occupies the realm of reality, or that of representation only. From Tatlin's corner reliefs and his insistence on productivism to the Earthworks of the 1970s, many twentieth-century sculptors have wanted to smash the glass bubble that encases sculpture in a world of illusion, representation, idealization. They wanted it to exist, to function, to act, in the field of the real. But they were fighting against all those interests—the museum, the art market, the idealizing aesthetic discourse—for which sculpture had to be seen as occupying not an actual but a virtual realm, a realm in which one confronted not a thing, but a representation. Throughout the century these interests continue to idealize sculpture; even while certain sculptors continue to fight that idealization. And many of these do so from within the logic of the desiring machine, the bachelor apparatus, the part-object.

*

Louise Bourgeois gave up painting in the late 1940s because, as she put it, she was "not satisfied with its level of reality."[6] Needing something to exist materially, something that would act in the physical world, she turned to sculpture. And, seeking what she called "fantastic reality," she sought the condition of the desiring machine.

Just before making this move she had produced a little booklet containing nine short stories (none longer than 75 words), each illustrated with an engraving, the book itself titled *He Disappeared into Complete Silence*. A typical story goes like this:

> Once a man was waving to his friend from the elevator.
> He was laughing so much that he stuck his head out and the
>   ceiling cut it off.

*

In writing the introduction for this work, Marius Bewley cautions against psychoanalytically projecting the stories and their accompanying images onto their maker. "It will be better to avoid any psycho-inquisitorial session," he says. But his discussion cannot avoid "the obvious pattern and tone of the stories" in which the plot and the affectless style repetitively stage the same "tiny tragedies" of human frustration:

> At the outset [he writes], someone is happy in the anticipation of an event or in the possession of something pleasing. In the end, his own happiness is destroyed either when he seeks to communicate it, or, perversely, seeks to deny the necessity for communication. The protagonists are miserable because they can neither escape the isolation

He Disappeared into Complete Silence, 1947. Engraving, 10 x 14 inches. Museum of Modern Art, New York; Alby Aldrich Rockefeller Fund.

which has become a condition of their own identities, nor yet accept it as wholly natural. Their attempts to free themselves, or accept their situation invariably end in disaster, for the first is impossible, and the second is abnormal. One man becomes a tragic figure when he discovers he cannot tell other people why he is happy. He tries, but nobody can understand his speech.[7]

Meditating on the stories' pattern of self-immurement and loss of communication, a drying up both of anything to say and any means of saying it, Bewley then comments on the engravings in which people are replaced by a rigid architectural landscape occupied by ladders, cranes, water towers, elevator shafts. It is an object-landscape, or, to relate it to the surrealist background from which it springs, a part-object-landscape. And the stories, in both the obsession that shapes their plots, and the mechanical flatness of their tone, sound like schizo-stories, the litanies of the bachelor apparatus. Is it necessary to say, that in speaking of the work in this way, one has not entered a "psycho-inquisitorial session"? Just as Beckett produces *Molloy*, Bourgeois produces *He Disappeared into Complete Silence*. Molloy makes a certain logic available, explores it, turns it round before the eyes of the reader; so does Bourgeois. And if she left drawing and painting for sculpture, it was to do this with even greater physical insistence.

In all the literature that exists on Bourgeois's work no word is ever breathed about Marcel Duchamp. It is as though the bachelor apparatus could have no resonance in her sculptural world. But Louise Bourgeois's sculpture began by projecting the architectural elements from *He Disappeared into Complete Silence* into three dimensions. In her first sculptures, the anthropomorphized building types yield to another kind of subarchitectural element, the carved entry post set up in tribal villages, known to anyone even slightly acquainted with African art. These composite "posts" as they emerged from Bourgeois's hands were given the status of subjects from the very first. In 1949 they were called things like *Portrait of C. Y.* or *Portrait of Jean-Louis* or *Observer*. But in 1950 they assumed a different type of title: *Figure Who Brings Bread, Figure Gazing at a House, Figure Leaving the House, Figures Who Talk to Each Other without Seeing Each Other.*

Portrait of Jean Louis, 1947–49. Painter wood, 34 3/4 x 3 7/8 x 2 1/8 inches. Mr. and Mrs. Keith L. Sachs Collection, Philadelphia.

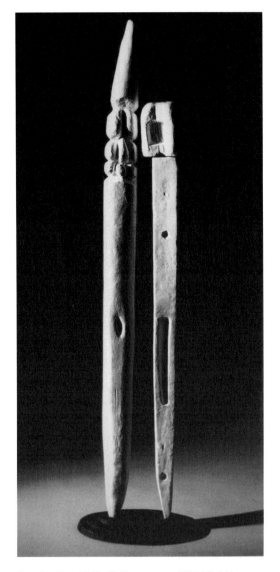

Listening One, 1947–49. Bronze, cast 1982, 79 1/4 x
11 1/4 x 4 1/2 inches. Galerie Lelong, Zurich.

And their installation made it clear that they were conceived of as functioning in groups. "The figures were presences," Bourgeois has said, "which needed the room, the six sides of the cube. . . . It was the reconstruction of the past."[8]

Duchamp's bachelor apparatus is also composed of figures typecast for roles in society—the postman, the stationmaster, the waiter, the carriage driver, the errand boy, etc. And these rigid personages, their heads shrunk to little points and knobs, rest immobile in their chariot singing their litanies. Another name for them could be "figures who talk to each other without seeing each other." They are not so much subjects, in the sense of individuals possessing independent consciousnesses, as agents within the process of the apparatus. They are a series of connections, the connections between desiring machines.

*

If writers about Louise Bourgeois's sculpture had, until just recently, fallen into the habit of calling it "abstract," this is partly because the critical *doxa* had made "abstraction" a form of praise, and partly because Bourgeois encouraged this attitude with statements like: "I am not particularly aware, or interested in, the erotic in my work. . . . I am exclusively concerned, at least consciously, with formal perfection. . . ."[9] But this tendency is the function of something else as well; it is the unanalyzed acknowledgment of the morphological ambivalence that grips the objects.

Take *Trani Episode* (1971–72), a work in which two flaccid ovoids, with pointed tips, are superposed, the top one at right angles to its mate. Lucy Lippard describes the strange internal contradiction of this work, calling it a phallic image that is "benign—fat, nestling, almost 'motherly,'" since as she says of the forms, "one has a nipple on the end, and both look like penises."[10] What she is pointing to is the constant impulse in Bourgeois's work to short-circuit the logic of form and to produce an unthinkable mutation within form in which oppositions are collapsed to produce what Georges Bataille has termed the *informe*.[11] Indeed, it is precisely in analyzing Bataille's novel *L'histoire de l'oeil* (1926) that Roland Barthes describes its manner of generating an experience of "round phallicism"—a transgression of that formal logic which depends on the distinction

Trani Episode, 1971. Plaster and latex, 23 1/4 x 23 1/4 x 17 inches. Robert Miller Gallery, New York.

of categorical oppositions, a transgression that thus produces the scandal of the erosion of form that is the *informe*.[12] It is this erosion of form that conduces a sense of the "abstract"—which is to say, the unlocatable—in Bourgeois's work. But this erosion does not involve that kind of attack on matter, that attempt to pulverize the very materials of sculpture, that characterized the antiform turn within the minimalism of the late 1960s. Rather it is a logical, categorical erosion. For "form" does not just mean physical shape. Rather it refers to the imposition of distinctions on the indistinctness of chaos—distinctions like inside/outside, figure/ground, male/female, living/dead. It is the transgression of these distinctions, the dangerous imagination of their collapse, that produces the *informe*.

It was also Bataille who demonstrated the way the logical categories of form did more than merely shape reality; even more important, it is through them that reality is given a meaning. All of reality is made to pass through the grid of those logical paradigms that, as structuralism has labored to show us, generate signification: high/low, self/other, organic/inorganic, nature/culture, noble/ignoble.

To situate oneself, or one's work, within the *informe* is once more to embrace the logic of *Anti-Oedipus,* the logic of the part-object. For in announcing themselves as "against Oedipus," Deleuze and Guattari are taking a stand against the assumption that the experience of desire must always be a desire for meaning, that Oedipus is the drive for symbolization, for representation, for the summoning forth of the signified. If the desiring machines produce, they do not produce meaning, representation, form. As we have already seen, what they produce is a flow for the next machine to process.

The logocentrism—the drive for symbolization, for meaning—of the structure of "Oedipus" was the target of Deleuze and Guattari's attack. This Oedipal logocentrism, rebaptized "phal-logocentrism"—in the light of the psychoanalytic position that the missing phallus is, as the first object of desire, the master signified, the driving force of the whole system of signification—is also the target of much feminism. When Luce Irigaray writes about "ce sexe qui n'en est pas un," she is addressing the scandal of female transgressiveness simultaneously against form—a decentered, amorphous, nonphallic experience of plea-sure—and against logos, or meaning.

The appeal of Louise Bourgeois's work for feminism is obvious and sure. And it is certainly the feminist pressure on the critical and art-historical establish-ment that has done the most to cry out against a construction of the modernist canon such that art such as Bourgeois's would not be given its rightful place. But what I would like to stress is that to honor Bourgeois in the way that would really pay her justice is to see how her work's roots had, from the beginning, spread in many directions within the art and thought of this century. They have always tapped into many logics that a hegemonic modernism has ignored, but that we can ignore no longer, particularly when we see how those logics com-bine into their own, powerfully emotive system: the part-object, the bachelor apparatus, the confabulations of *art brut,* the *informe,* the desiring machines. Bourgeois has been the master of all of this, and that for over four decades.

—Paris, 1989

Agnes Martin: The /Cloud/

Do you remember the hilarity, as a child, of playing the game that takes the form: if you were a vegetable (or a color, an animal, etc.), what vegetable (color, animal) would you be? The surrealists were fond of rewriting children's games in the register of adult desire. I remembered that when I stumbled on the information that Agnes Martin had made a film. Agnes Martin? A film? If you were Agnes Martin, I thought, and you made a film, what film would it be?

Zorns Lemma, I thought.

In order to achieve its peculiar transubstantiation of matter, Hollis Frampton's great film reorganizes both the real world of cinema's photographic support and the temporal dimension of its continuous unreeling into the atemporal, nonspatial order of the grid. *Zorns Lemma* (1970) is, for that reason, profoundly abstract. As its one-second-long shots present us with the regular beat of disjunctive bits of reality, each one bearing a word discovered in the urban landscape beginning with the letter appropriate to its place in the alphabetic organization of the work, a linguistic matrix seems to settle over the visual field. Cycling again and again over the alphabetic ground—*eagle . . . hair . . . wagon . . . yacht*—the film gradually replaces each "letter" with a fragment of landscape that in this arbitrary play of substitutions takes on the character of a pure emblem, the insubstantiality of an idea. Indeed the first four substitute images—reeds, smoke, flames, waves—capture a thought of the real as primordial separation: earth, air, fire, water. And behind that separation, as its very condition of being, is light.

Zorns Lemma ends with a long stationary shot of two people in a snowy field, with their dog, walking away from the camera and toward a stand of trees in the distance. As the image is increasingly absorbed by the continuous whiteness of the snow-struck frame, the sound track completes the reading of a text by the thirteenth-century theologian Robert Grosseteste, called *On Light, or the Ingression of Forms*. "In the beginning of time," it says, "light drew out matter along with itself into a mass as great as the fabric of the world." And at another point it says, "Matter cannot be emptied of form; form is light itself, and the bringer of dimensions into matter."

Gabriel, for this is the name of Martin's film, also watches the movement of a subject through nature, in this case silently tracking a young boy walking through a mountain landscape in the American West. Martin made this film in 1976, two years into her renewed involvement with painting, having left New York and art behind her in 1967, only to begin again in 1974 in New Mexico. An hour and twenty minutes long, *Gabriel* was screened at the Institute of Contemporary Art in Philadelphia with a certain amount of fanfare in April 1977, and subsequently shown at White Columns, New York (1982). It is not a work Martin herself gives any indication of wanting to bracket away from the rest of her art.

Yet it should be. For *Gabriel* constructs a reading of Martin's own work as crypto-landscape, a reading that, since it is produced by the artist herself, tends to carry the weight of interpretive proof. The terrain of the work, in both film and painting, it seems to say, is that of the abstract sublime, behind which, underwriting it as its field of relevance, is the immensity, the endlessness, the ecstasy, the *terribilitá* of nature.

Gabriel begins with a shot of the boy seen from behind. He is staring at a vastness of sky, water, and beach, which fills the frame with six luminous horizontal bands of color. He does this, motionless, for a very long time: Caspar David Friedrich's *Monk by the Sea*. He then begins to walk, with the camera following close behind, moving steadily upward along a mountain stream. At a certain point in this ascent the camera passes beyond him to capture the target of his gaze—revealing in shot after shot, each one held for a very long time, one after another "Agnes Martin" painting: a turquoise river filling the frame with a rushing, transparent luminosity vertically laced by the burnished whiteness of stalks of sage; the all-over pattern of aquamarine shallows washing over the nearly uniform indistinctness of a ground of pebbles; the horizontal bands of a falls dividing into green, white, brown, white, green, white.

There is aid and assistance in all of this for the kind of reading of Martin's painting that was initiated early on by Lawrence Alloway, in the catalogue of Martin's 1973 retrospective, and has continued ever since. This reading comprehends the canvases as analogues of nature, "both," as Alloway wrote, "by inference from her imagery and from judging her titles."[1] And indeed, like the film *Gabriel,* Martin's titles have always held out an invitation to experience the work as an allusion to nature: *The Beach, Desert, Drops, Earth, Field, Garden, Happy Valley, Islands, Leaf in the Wind, Milk River, Night Sea, Orange Grove, Wheat, White Stone, Falling Blue.*

Nonetheless Alloway is careful, in his text, to acknowledge all those admonitions Martin herself has always pronounced against understanding her work as an abstracted nature: "My paintings have neither objects, nor space, nor time, not anything—no forms," he quotes her saying. Or again, he cautions, "Referring to one of her poems she notes: 'This poem, like the paintings, is not really about nature. It is not what is seen. It is what is known forever in the mind.'"[2]

It is one thing, however, to listen to Martin insisting, "My work is anti-nature," and it is another to hold this claim steady as one approaches her paintings. Alloway's reading became the standard for interpreting Martin, as the rubric "abstract sublime" slid into the space between her work and its succession of interpreter/viewers. Characteristically, Carter Ratcliff referred Martin's work to Edmund Burke's *Inquiry on the Sublime* which, in the mid–eighteenth century, laid down a recipe for satisfying the growing taste for "sublime effects," turning on ways the artist could produce a sense of limitlessness by abandoning the measure parceled out by traditional modes of composition and working instead with forms "melted as it were into each other." Burke's description of "a perfect simplicity, an absolute uniformity in disposition, shape and coloring," his call for a succession "of uniform parts" that can permit "a comparatively small quantity of matter to produce a grander effect than a much larger quantity disposed in another manner" seemed made for Martin's work, just as that work—as paired down and simplified as it might appear—could be thought nonetheless to smuggle within it diffused references to the repertory of natural "subjects" that followed from Burke's analysis: "the sea (Turner), the sky (Constable), foliage (Church) and, simply, light."[3]

It is this covert allusion to nature that the category *abstract sublime* has come to imply, with the abstract work always able to be decoded by its romantic double: Rothko read out through Friedrich; Pollock by Turner's storms; Martin by Turner's skies.[4]

But again it has consistently been Martin herself who has cautioned against a romantic context for her work. Repeating that she sees herself joined to an ancient tradition of classicists—"Coptic, Egyptian, Greek, Chinese"—she defines this tradition as something that turns its back on nature. "Classicism forsakes the nature pattern," she writes.[5] "Classicists are people that look out with their back to the world/ It represents something that isn't possible in the world/ More perfection than is possible in the world/ It's as unsubjective as possible. . . . The point—it doesn't exist in the world."[6]

And this same text, written three years before Martin made *Gabriel,* contains an extraordinary condemnation of the trope at work in her own film: "The classic is cool/ a classical period/ it is cool because it is impersonal/ the detached and impersonal/ If a person goes walking in the mountains that is not detached/ and impersonal, he's just looking back."

*

In the exceedingly superficial and repetitive literature on Agnes Martin, there is one arresting exception. It is Kasha Linville's careful phenomenological reading in which for the first and only time there is a description of what it is actually like to see the paintings, which, she explains, "are sequences of illusions of textures that change as viewing distance changes.[7]

First there is the close-to reading, in which one is engaged in the work's facture and drawing, in the details of its materiality in all their sparse precision: the irregular weave of the linen, the thickness and uniformity of the gesso, the touch in the application of the penciled lines. "Sometimes," Linville explains,

> her line is sharp, as in an early painting, *Flower in the Wind,* 1963. Sometimes its own shadow softens it—that is, it is drawn once beneath the pigment or gesso and then redrawn on top, as in *The Beach.* Most often, her line respects the canvas grain, skimming its surface without filling the low places in the fabric so it becomes almost a dotted or broken line at close range. Sometimes she uses pairs of lines that dematerialize as rapidly as the lighter-drawn single ones. As you move back from a canvas like *Mountain II,* 1966, the pairs become single, gray horizontals and then begin to disappear.[8]

But this "moving back" from the matrix of the fine grids of Martin's 1960–67 work, as well as from the more grossly calibrated bands of her post-1974 painting, is a crucial second "moment" in the viewing of the work. For here is where the ambiguities of illusion take over from the earlier materiality of a surface redoubled by the weave of Martin's grids or bands; and it is at this place that the paintings go atmospheric. Again, Linville's description of this effect is elegant and precise. "I don't mean 'atmosphere' in the spatially illusionistic sense I associate with color field painting," she writes. "Rather it is a non-radiating, impermeable mist. It feels like, rather than looks like atmosphere. Somehow, the red lines [she is speaking here of *Red Bird*] dematerialize the canvas, making it hazy, velvety. Then, as you step back even further, the painting closes down entirely, becoming completely opaque."

That opaqueness of the third "moment," produced by a fully distant, more objective vantage on the work, brackets the atmospheric interval of the middle-distance view, closing it from behind, so to speak. Wall-like and impenetrable, this view now disperses the earlier "atmosphere." And this final result, as Linville again writes of Martin, is "to make her paintings impermeable, immovable as stone."

Flower in the Wind, 1963. Oil on canvas, 75 x 75 inches.

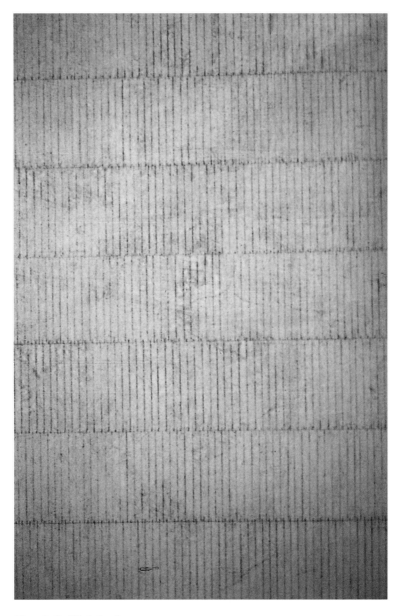

Flower in the Wind, detail.

———

The "abstract sublime" consideration of Martin's art, never so careful or accurate as this one, implies that *atmosphere* or *light* are a given of the paintings, which, like a certain kind of landscape subject—clouds, sea, fields—can simply be observed from any vantage one might take on them. The landscape subject, no matter how reduced or abstracted, simply defines the work, is an objective attribute of it, like the color blue, or red. But Linville's three distances make it clear that /atmosphere/ is an effect set within a system in which an opposite effect is also at work, and that it both defines and is defined by that opposite.[9] Linville's three distances, that is, transform the experience from an intuition into a system, and convert *atmosphere* from a signified (the content of an image) into a signifier—/atmosphere/—the open member of a differential series: wall/mist; weave/cloud; closed/open; form/formless.

*

By a curious coincidence, it was just when Linville was noticing Martin's production of the three distances that Hubert Damisch was completing his study *Théorie du /nuage/,* a book that rewrites the history of Renaissance and Baroque painting according to a system in which the signifier /cloud/ plays a major, foundational role.[10] This role, which is that of a "remainder"—the thing that cannot be fitted into a system but which nevertheless the system needs in order to constitute itself *as* a system—finds its most perfect illustration in the famous demonstration performed by Brunelleschi at the opening of the fifteenth century, the demonstration that both invented and supplied the complete theory of perspective.

Having painted the image of the baptistery in Florence on a wooden panel into which a tiny peephole had been drilled at the exact vanishing point of the perspective construction, Brunelleschi devised an apparatus for viewing this image. Its reverse side would be placed up against the brow of the observer, whose eye, right at the peephole, would gaze through the panel, while in front of the panel, at arm's length, the observer would hold up a mirror. The depicted baptistery, reflected in this mirror, would thus be guaranteed a "correct" viewing according to the theory of perspective's *legitimate construction,* in which the

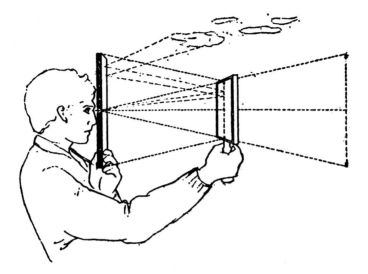

Reconstruction of Brunelleschi's first perspective experiment, as reproduced in Hubert Damisch, *Théorie du /nuage/* (Paris: Le Seuil, 1972).

vanishing point and viewing point must be geometrically synonymous. In this sense the representation is the function not of one but of two constructed planes: that of the "viewer" (stationary, mono-ocular) and that of the display (constructed in terms of measurable bodies deployed in space, thus capable of being submitted to the determinations of geometry).

But between those two planes of the perspective apparatus something was necessarily added, slipped into the construction as though it were a measurable, definable body, but which gave the lie nonetheless to this very possibility of definition. This something was the /cloud/. For the sky above the baptistery on Brunelleschi's panel was not depicted in paint; rather the area given over to it was executed in silver leaf so that, acting as a mirror, it would capture onto its surface the reflections of the real sky passing over the head of the viewer staring into the optical box of the perspective construction.

Perspective was thus understood from the first to be a matter of architectonics, of a structure built from delimited bodies standing in a specific space and possessing a contour defined by lines. The immeasurability and ubiquity of the sky, however, and the unanalyzable surfacelessness of the clouds render these things fundamentally unknowable by the perspective order. "The process to which Brunelleschi had recourse for 'showing' the sky," Damisch writes,

> this way of mirroring that he inserted into the pictorial field like a piece of marquetry and onto which the sky and its clouds were captured, this mirror is thus much more than a subterfuge. It has the value of an epistemological emblem . . . to the extent that it reveals the limitations of the perspective code, for which the demonstration furnishes the complete theory. It makes perspective appear as a structure of exclusions, whose coherence is founded on a series of refusals that nonetheless must make a place, as the background onto which it is printed, for the very thing it excludes from its order.[11]

It is in this sense that painting understands its scientific aspirations—toward measurement, toward the probing of bodies, toward exact knowledge—as always being limited or conditioned by the unformed, which is unknowable and unrepresentable. And if the /architectural/ came to symbolize the reach of the artist's "knowledge," the /cloud/ operated as the lack in the center of that knowledge, the outside that joins the inside in order to constitute it as an inside.

Thus before being a thematic element—functioning in the moral and allegorical sphere as a registration of miraculous vision, or of ascension, or as the opening onto divine space; or in the psychological sphere as an index of desire, fantasy, hallucination; or, for that matter, before being a visual integer, the image of vaporousness, instability, movement—the /cloud/ is a differential marker in a semiological system. This can be seen for example in the extent to which cloud elements are interchangeable within the repertory of religious imagery. "The fact that an object can thus be substituted for another in the economy of the sacred visual text," Damisch writes, "this fact is instructive: the /cloud/ has no meaning that can be properly assigned to it; it has no other value than that which comes to it from those serial relations of opposition and substitution that it entertains with the other elements of the system."[12]

Meaning, according to this argument, is then a function of a system that underpins and produces it, a system—/cloud/ vs. /built, definable space/—with its own autonomy, that of painting, which precedes the specifics of either theme or image.

*

Autonomy, of course, has come by now to have indescribably bad associations; like formalism, it is thought to be the blinkered product of ideological construction. Yet much art has been produced within this ideology and in relation to a conception of autonomy; and the rush to move beyond the circumscribed aesthetic sphere to the *hors texte,* the context, the legitimating "real" text, often produces superficial readings, as in the case of leaching out Agnes Martin's painting into the concealed landscapes of the "abstract sublime."

But if we allow ourselves for a moment to entertain this transgressive thought of autonomy, we come upon a position, itself the founding moment of art history as a discipline, that sets up, along with Damisch's, a model for Agnes

---

Martin's three distances. This is the work Alois Riegl developed over the course of his *Stilfragen* (1893) and *Spätrömische Kunstindustrie* (1901), studies that fend off all hypotheses about the putative effect of external factors on art's development—whether in the material field, as in Semper's theories of art's genesis out of building practices; or in the field of the "real," as theories of mimesis would have it; or due to the contingencies of history, as the "barbaric invasions" explanation of the supposed decline in late Roman art would imply. Instead, Riegl posits an entirely internal or autonomous evolution, one that continues without gap or deflection from the most ancient civilizations of the Near East up through Byzantium.

This evolution, "dialectic" in nature, arises from the desire, externalized via art, to grasp things in the most objective way possible, untainted, that is, by the merely happenstance and contingent vantage point of the viewing subject. But in acknowledging the object in terms of almost any level of sculptural relief (that is, in promoting an experience of its tactility), shadow is necessarily admitted into the confines of the object—shadow which, marking the position of the spectator relative to the object, is the very index of subjectivity. "The art of antiquity," Riegl wrote, "which sought as much as possible to enclose the figures in objective, tactile borders, accordingly was bound from the very beginning to include a subjective, optical element; this, however, gave rise to a contradiction, the resolution of which was to pose a problem. Every attempt to solve this problem led in turn to a new problem, which was handed down to the next period, and one might well say that the entire art history of the ancient world consists of a developmental chain made up of such problems and their solutions."[13]

The development Riegl charts goes from what he calls the haptic objectivism of the Greeks—the delineation of the clarity of the object through an appeal to and a stimulation of the tactile associations of the viewer—to the optical objectivism of Roman art—in which the need to set the figure up in space as radically freestanding led to the projection of the rear side of the body and hence the use of the drill to excavate the relief plane. It arrives finally at the most extreme moment of this opticalism carried out in the service of the object. When the relief plane itself becomes the "object" whose unity must be preserved, this leads, in examples Riegl drew on from late Roman decorative arts, to the construction of the object itself in terms of a kind of moiré effect, with a constant oscillation between figure and ground depending—and here is where this begins to get interesting for Agnes Martin—on where the viewer happens to be standing. Writing that now "the ground is the interface," Riegl describes the fully optical play of this phenomenon once what had formerly been background emerges as *object:* "The relationship of the bronze buckle alters with each movement of its wearer; what was just now the light-side can become at the next moment shadow-side."[14]

Since this figure/ground fluctuation varies with the stance of the viewer one might argue that the object, now fully dependent upon its perceiver, has become entirely subjectivized. And indeed, although Riegl argues that this development ultimately gave rise to the subjective as a newly autonomous problem for the history of art, one that would fulfill itself in the efforts, for example, of seventeenth-century Dutch portraitists to portray something as nonobjective as states of attention, he does not read this late Roman moment as itself subjective. Rather, he wants to argue, with this optical glitter organized into the very weft of the object, it is the subject-viewer who has been fractured, having now been deprived of the security of a unitary vantage. This is still the *Kunstwollen* of objectivism at work, but in the highest throes of its dialectical development. The filigrees of late Roman relief, far from being a regression to a more ancient or barbaric linearism, are the sublation of this aesthetic problem. "The screw of time has seemingly turned all the way back to its old position," Riegl writes, "yet in reality it has ended up one full turn higher."[15]

*

Agnes Martin's claim to be a classical artist—along with the full complement of Egyptians, Greeks, and Copts who make up Riegl's objectivist *Kunstwollen*—has been in the main disbelieved by her interpreters. How can her interest in formlessness, it is argued, be reconciled with such a claim, given classicism's complete commitment to form? When Martin observes, approvingly, "You wouldn't think of form by the ocean," or when she says that her work is about "merging, about formlessness, breaking down form," this is thought to under-write the idea that she has transcended classicism for a newly ardent and romantic attitude toward the sublime.

Yet let us take Martin at her word and allow her affiliations to a classicism that, in Riegl's terms, would commit her to an objectivist vision, no matter how optically fractured, and to a place within a development internal to the system of art, a system within which the marker /cloud/ has a foundational role to play.

This objectivism, unfolding within the twentieth century, would itself have to be seamed into the fully subjectivist project that was put in place follow-ing the Renaissance, a Cartesian project that has only intensified steadily into the present. Except that at the beginning of the century, modernist painting opened up, within an ever growing dependence of the work on the phenome-nology of seeing (and thus on the subject), what we could call an "objectivist opticality," namely, an attempt to discover—at the level of pure abstraction—the objective conditions, or the logical grounds of possibility, for the purely sub-jective phenomenon of vision itself.

It is in this context that the grid achieves its historical importance: as the transformer that moved painting from the subjective experience of the empirical field to the internal grounds of what could be called subjectivity as such, subjec-tivity now construed as a logic. Because the grid not only displays perfectly the conditions of what could be called the *visual*—the simultaneity of vision's grasp of its field dissolving the spatial (tactile) separation of figure *against* ground into the continuous immediacy of a purely optical spread—but also repeats the origi-nal, antique terms of a desire for objectivity and extreme clarity. Like the Egyp-tian relief, the grid both enforces a shadowless linearity and is projected as though seen from no vantage at all. At least this is so in what could be called the classical period of the modernist grid, for which Mondrian would stand as the prime figure.

Let us say further that this attempt to grasp the logical conditions of vision was, like the dialectic of the ancient drive toward the utterly independent object, continually forced to include its opposite. For as the grid came to coincide more and more closely with its material support and to begin to actually depict the warp and weft of textiles (not only in Annie Albers's work, but in that of a host of followers such as Al Jensen), this supposed "logic of vision" became infected by the tactile. Two of the possible outcomes of this tactilization of what I've been calling an "objectivist opticality" are (1) to materialize the grid itself, as when Ellsworth Kelly constructs the network of *Colors for a Large Wall* out of sixty-four separate canvases (nonetheless retaining the optical or the indefinite in the form of chance);[16] or (2) to make the optical a function of the tactile (kinesthetic) field of its viewer, that is to say, the succession of those viewing distances the observer might assume. This latter is the case with Agnes Martin. And in her work it also remains clear that the optical, here marked as /cloud/, emerges within a system defined by being bracketed by its two materialist and tactile counterterms: the fabric of the grid in the near position and the wall-like stela of the impassive, perfectly square panel in the distant view. It is this closed system, taken as a whole, which preserves—like the moiré belt buckle—the drive toward the "objective," which is to say the fundamental classicism of its *Kunstwollen.*

To say all of this is, of course, impossibly outmoded, formalist, determinist, empty. But the /cloud/ remains bracketed within its peculiar system; and it is what Agnes Martin painted for these last thirty years. She destroyed all the rest.

—Paris, 1993

EVA HESSE: CONTINGENT

Although there are many ways to characterize the New York art world of the 1960s, all of them would probably focus on the same central experience, that of a small, private company gone suddenly, euphorically, dizzyingly public. The economic aspects of that image are, of course, appropriate. The consolidation of the stylistic hegemony of the New York School converted a provincial bohemia into a boomtown, a center of self-confident aesthetic energy on which there was lavished money, glamour, attention. But besides its economic connotations, the term *public* also carries the notion of discourse, of a collective language about the aims, ideals, and even rules of a given enterprise, the conversion of a merely private preoccupation into a discipline.

Discourse is the medium of, the support for, a public dialogue; and the 1960s was the time during which not only American critics but also many artists began, with a new articulateness and power, to write and to speak. Since the nature of this speech was public, the vehicle used for this discourse was that of the art magazines, of which one in particular seemed by the mid-1960s to concentrate this speech most insistently, and that one—*Artforum*—for a time became the center and the medium of art world discourse.

In May 1970 Eva Hesse entered that world of discourse through one simple stroke: an image of her work *Contingent* filled the cover of *Artforum,* and a relatively unknown artist was suddenly acknowledged as having a voice of extraordinary authority. Of all the works generated through the decade of the sixties, *Contingent* is surely one of the most masterful and moving, and it was this mastery and expressiveness that was immediately revealed through the color reproduction on that cover, an instantaneous recognition that surely could never have happened had it not been prepared for by ten years of public debate. Authority is the consequence of discourse, of the setting up of a problematic within and against which a dominant voice can establish itself. Authority cannot be a merely private affair.

But here we move into one of the many paradoxes that characterize the work of Eva Hesse. For the voice of authority that spoke through the image of *Contingent* was delivering the message of privacy, of a retreat from language, of a withdrawal into those extremely personal reaches of experience that are beyond, or beneath, speech.

The human voice makes sounds. These sounds, we could say, are mere acoustical matter. In order for that matter even to begin to perform the function of language it must be segmented, cut up into those distinct portions that will serve as the carriers, the formal integers of a given speech. English, for example, discards many of the glottal sounds that other languages retain. So for English speakers these sounds exist at the level of raw acoustical matter, at what is practically the condition of noise. What the image of *Contingent* was delivering to the art world was a declaration about the expressive power of matter itself, of matter held down to a level of the subarticulate. In art-historical terms we could say that *Contingent* was countering the formalist dialogue of the 1960s with the message of expressionism.

That, we could say, is the legacy of Eva Hesse's work—the thing she communicated to the generation that followed her—and if one speaks of legacy here, one does so literally, for the month of Hesse's entry into the consciousness of a wider public for art was the month of her death at the age of thirty-four. Hesse's expressionism, manifested through an experience of matter itself, had the liberating quality of Dr. Johnson's kicking the stone and crying, out of exasperation over the bottomless idealism of Berkeley's argument, "I refute it *thus*." Hesse's

Contingent, 1969. Fiberglass, polyester resin, and latex over cheesecloth, each of eight units, 114–168 x 36–48 inches. Australian National Gallery, Canberra.

expressionism carried the message that by kicking hard into the stone of inert matter, one would break through to an experience of the self, a self that will imprint its image into the heart of that matter.

Another way of saying this is that although Hesse's work takes the form of large expanses of dense coagulations and snarls of matter—of latex, of fiberglass, of cord, of plastic—the impression that forms through that matter is one of an extraordinary originality, as though this matter, in its preformal condition, were a reflection of the self as unmediated, preformalized origin, as the purest and most authentic source of feeling. The authority of *Contingent* derived from its assertion of originality, and the claim it made for the aesthetics of originary experience, of the self as origin. Most of the rhetoric that surrounds Hesse's work returns again and again to this experience of it as personal, private, original.

But here again, with this claim and our assent to it—for *Contingent's* affective quality does lie in its originality—we approach another of the paradoxes of Hesse's work. For Hesse's art depends, to an extreme degree, on the aesthetic discourse of the 1960s, on that public debate through which the notions of minimalism were articulated both in writing and in objects: notions of serial order and modular repetition; notions of architectural scale and scaffolding, by means of lattices and grids. *Sans II* (1968), Hesse's monumental, modular frieze is unthinkable without the precedents of Donald Judd, Carl Andre, and Ellsworth Kelly. *Accretion* (1968), with its repetition of tubular poles leaning against a wall, and *Vinculum I* (1969), in which a slablike form is also positioned by leaning, are both conditioned by certain minimalist objects—one thinks of the leaning slabs of John McCracken or of Dan Flavin's installations of fluorescent tubing. *Accession II* (1969), a five-sided cube, its interior tufted with rubber tubing, begins in the work of Judd, Robert Morris, and most important, Sol LeWitt. And with *Hang Up* (1966), the empty, six-foot, swaddled frame from which a single line of wrapped metal loops out onto the floor, we feel not only the experience of Flavin's open, luminous corner frames, but behind that, Jasper Johns's ironic display of the "empty" stretcher in *Canvas* (1956) or his projection of wire elements from flat, wall-like surfaces in work like *No* (1961) or *In Memory of My Feelings* (1961).

Accession II, 1969. Galvanized steel and plastic tubing, 30 3/4 x 30 3/4 x 30 3/4 inches.
Detroit Institute of Arts, Founders Society Purchase.

Just as the minimalist aspect of John's work—the gray surfaces, muffled by encaustic, the literalizing of flatness, the use of repetition—was important to Hesse's aesthetic, the other aspect of it that was continuous with certain strains in a Pop, antiformalist rhetoric was also available to her. Hesse's work was given a necessary kind of permission by the soft sculpture of Claes Oldenburg and by the obsessional and sadomasochistic imagery and forms of Lucas Samaras. Hesse herself seems to have been rather unselfconscious about declaring a relationship to the work of other artists. Had this not been the case she would probably not have felt as free as she was to lavish the kind of patience and care that was necessary to the production of her ink and wash modular drawings of 1966 and 1967 without being blocked by the problem of "influence" from the work of Agnes Martin. Or again, speaking of the hanging fiberglass skeins of *Right After* (1969), she felt free to acknowledge the importance of Jackson Pollock to her own thinking: "This piece is very ordered. Maybe I'll make it more structured, maybe I'll leave it changeable. When it's completed, its order could be chaos. Chaos can be structured as non-chaos. That we know from Jackson Pollock." And indeed, in the year following *Right After,* Hesse pushed deeper into the territory of Pollock's "chaos" with another hanging skein work, this time in snarls of latex-covered rope (*Untitled* 1970). Thus, the paradox of Hesse's originality: how is an oeuvre so visibly built on the armature of a predominantly minimalist discourse to be simply termed "original"?

If we wish to come to grips with this problem we must, I think, return to *Contingent* and the experience of its authority. That is, we must remember that authority can only arise as a function of discourse. For all that *Contingent*'s projection of the expressive power of raw matter tended to eclipse its relation to the terms of an extremely codified aesthetic discourse, it was that relationship, operating within the work, that was the ultimate guarantor of its immediate position of authority.

Contingent is made of eight bannerlike elements that hang from ceiling to floor. Each of the elements suspends a large, rectangular stretch of latex-covered cheesecloth within a translucent field of fiberglass. The banners hang parallel to one another and at right angles to the wall. In those flattened, rectilinear stretches

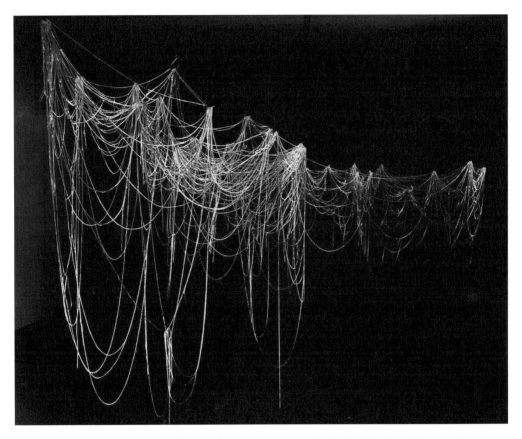

Right After, 1969. Casting resin over fiberglass cord and wire hooks, 60 x 216 x 48 inches. Milwaukee Art Museum, Gift of Friends of Art.

of fabric there is an ineluctable reference to the surface and format of painting. Further, through the experience of light and color that *Contingent* generates as its condition or ambiance, we feel ourselves to be in the affective terrain of painting. But *Contingent* is not a painting. And this is so because its flattened fields are not parallel but at right angles to the wall. Faced with the spread of *Contingent,* what we see is a series of edges: the edges of planes that self-evidently occupy the real space in which they hang.

Within the problematics of painting this particular experience of edge would be produced, for example, by a museum where, through some caprice of the curator, a group of, say, Rembrandts has been installed at a ninety-degree angle to the wall so that as the viewer faces the works all he or she could really see would be the sides of their frames. In this hypothetical case the paintings, the Rembrandts, would have been rendered "useless," their normal function—that of making a certain order of things visible—annulled; and instead we would be given the extra-pictorial anomaly of the painting-object, or the painting-as-object. We would see, that is, the objecthood of the object (the painting-object) eclipsing its "use."

I have given these rotated Rembrandts as a hypothetical case, one that we could imagine but could never imagine ourselves really being asked to see. Yet within the practice of sixteenth- and seventeenth-century art, there were in fact concrete instances of something like the scene I have been projecting. These cases fall under the general term anamorphosis, of which Holbein's painting, *The Ambassadors,* is the most celebrated example. The devices at work in this painting are well known. To look at the painting is to see spread before one representations of earthly riches and power, and at the same time to be perplexed by a large, amorphous, and unreadable form that occupies a diagonal area at the feet of those worldly emissaries. Only by moving ninety degrees away from one's normal vantage onto the painting and stationing oneself at its edge, is one able to foreshorten and contract the amorphous spread of that form and to see that it is a skull, a death's head, a memento mori. Other paintings that include such a memento mori do so without requiring the viewer to gyrate around the work in the way Holbein does; the death's head is shown as continuous with the system of visibility that presents all the rest of the contents of a given painting to view. But Holbein's *Ambassadors* is precisely about the eclipse of that system of visibility. It insists that there are two different, mutually exclusive vantages: the one within the world from which death is not visible; and the one outside, or at an angle to it, from which death is seen because the "world" is not. And what *is* continually seen in the *Ambassadors* is precisely the condition of this mutual eclipse.

There is a way in which *Contingent*'s own double perspective is something like that of anamorphosis. From the front, the view is of the elements' edges with their sculptural condition eclipsing that of the pictorial; from a raking angle, one's perception is of the surfaces of the banners and the planarity of the rectangular fields, a perception that foregrounds the pictorial aspect of the experience. The problematic here is obviously very different from that of Holbein's *Ambassadors*. In *Contingent,* as in Hesse's work in general, the issue is that of the mutual eclipse of the conventions, or institutions, of painting and sculpture as separate modalities of experience.

The discourse of sixties aesthetics had of course been leading in this direction. It had been focused on justifying or legitimating the internal structure of a given work—a structure made visible by the articulations of a surface by drawing or of a three-dimensional object by the separation of its parts—by means other than those of mimesis or illusion. In this way the minimalist aesthetic came to be deeply engaged with the condition of the literal, with the purging of illusion from the work of art by making everything about it external. Illusionism depends on the convention of the "inside" of a work of art, on a space it does not share with that of the rest of the world. Literalism was an attempt to make the work, whether sculpture or painting, stop at its surface. In order to do this, all divisions of the surface had to be experienced as the actual separations of the material of the surface: for example, the colored areas in a painting by Ellsworth Kelly change because the canvas panel that bears a given color literally comes to an end and another one begins; or again, the "drawing" in a floor sculpture by Carl

Andre is a real function of the separateness of each square or tile of metal. More than anything else minimalism was focused on surface, and where the surface stops, which is edge.

The most powerful and continuous element of Eva Hesse's work comes from the way it concentrates on this condition of edge, the way it makes the edge more affective and imperious by materializing it. In this way, the edge that is displayed by Hesse is not focused on the boundaries *within* a painting or a sculpture, but rather on the boundary that lies *between* the institutions of painting and sculpture. In the language of anamorphosis, we could say we are positioned at the edge from which the meaning of death is understood literally as the condition of the world disappearing from view.

In Hesse's work the gravitational field of either painting or sculpture is always experienced as shifting. Things begin on the wall and end on the floor, or on the wall adjacent to the one where they started. Things lean from floor to wall; or they begin stretched out on the horizontal plane only to turn the corner and snake up onto the vertical one. This focus on the boundaries, on what is at the edges of either an object or a convention, is what Hesse shares with the discourse out of which she made her art. But where she carried her art to a point at some distance from that discourse was in showing that from the position at the edge—the boundary between those two formalized conventions—there emerges an experience of matter that is both bewildering and beautiful.

Hesse's work is in that sense a kind of reinvention for her own time of the anamorphotic condition: the condition in which form and matter are given the real possibility of eclipsing one another, and within which one experiences the pity and terror of that eclipse.

—New York, 1979

CINDY SHERMAN: UNTITLED

THE FILM STILLS

Some people have told me they remember the film that one of my images is derived from, but in fact I had no film in mind at all.

—Cindy Sherman[1]

Here is a curious story: an art critic writes an account of Cindy Sherman presenting her work to an art school audience. She shows slides of her "film stills"—the black and white photographs in which as both director and actress she projects a range of 1950s screen images—and next to each, he reports, she presents the real movie stills on which her own images were based. What emerges through this comparison, he says, is that "virtually every detail seemed to be accounted for: right down to the buttons on the blouses, the cropping of the image, even the depth of field of the camera."[2]

Although he is upset by what this comparison reveals about the slavishness of Sherman's procedure—the stroke-for-stroke meticulousness of the copy, so to speak—he is certain that what Sherman is after when we encounter these *Stills* is in any case a recognition of the original, although not as a source waiting to be replicated, but rather as a memory waiting to be summoned. So he speaks about the viewer of the normally unaccompanied Sherman *Still* "starting to recall the original film image." And, he says, "if it wasn't the actual film" the viewer recalled, "then it was an ad for it; and if not that, then it was a picture from a review in a newspaper."

On its face this story is amazing. Because in a Sherman *Film Still* there is no "original." Not in the "actual film," nor in a publicity shot or "ad," nor in any other published "picture." The condition of Sherman's work in the *Stills*—and part of their point, we could say—is the simulacral nature of what they contain, its condition of being a copy *without* an original.

The structure of the simulacrum, then, along with Sherman's exploration of it, is something that needs to be examined. But even before doing so, it is worth staying with the story of the slide show and its putative unveiling of an "original," which is to say the story's blatant, screaming, *Rashomon*-like, misrecognition.

Did Sherman ever show real movie stills next to her own work? And if so, to what end? Since her own images manage their projection of a whole array of stereotypical Hollywood or New Wave heroines, along with the very atmospheres through which they are cast—the *film noir*'s hard-bitten denizen of the night, one of Hitchcock's plucky but vulnerable career girls, the B-movie's small-town innocent swamped by Metropolis, a New Wave vehicle of alienated despair, and so on—and yet do all of this from within a kind of intense, generalized memory, what would a comparison of, say, a still from a Douglas Sirk film and a Cindy Sherman mean? Could it indicate that the sense that the two images intersect—no matter how distant their actual details might be—derives from the way *both* Sherman and Sirk (in addition to Sirk's actress) are each imaginatively focused on a remembered fantasy—the *same* remembered fantasy—of a character, who is "herself" not only fictional, but, like Emma Bovary, the creature as well of fiction, a character woven from the tissue of all the romances she has ever consumed? Could it mean that with the stereotypes projected by these fictions, with regard to the creatures of this fantasized romance, could it mean that these boxes-within-boxes of seeming "memory" always produce what

Untitled Film Still #32, 1979. Silver print, 8 x 10 inches.

appears to be an authentic copy, even though there is no "real" original to be found? So that Sirk's copy and Sherman's copy uncannily overlap like two search-lights probing through the night toward the same vaguely perceived target? Let's speculate that this is why Sherman would show her own image and, say, Sirk's.

Why, then, would the critic misrecognize the comparison, making one a copy and the other an original: Sherman, the artist, copying the "real" of the Hollywood film? Roland Barthes, the structuralist critic, would have a word with which to explain this strange hallucination; and that word would be *myth:* the art critic who "saw" the comparison as replication—*Untitled, Film Still* = image taken from real film—was in the grip of myth, consuming it, Barthes would say.

Barthes would, of course, be using the term *myth* in a somewhat limited, rather technical way. And if it is useful to explain how he deploys the term, it's because myth is also what Sherman herself is analyzing and projecting in *Untitled, Film Stills.* Although not as a myth consumer, like the critic; but rather as a my-thographer, like Barthes—a demystifier of myth, a de-myth-ifier.

To consume a myth is to buy a package along with the salesman's pitch. The salesman's pitch names it, and the buyer, never looking under the hood, accepts the name, is satisfied (or suckered) by the pitch. The somewhat more technical analysis involves the terms *signified* and *signifier,* or form and content. It goes like this: a schoolchild reads in a grammar book *quia ego nominor leo.*[3] The signifiers of this string of words are the letters—the material component of the composite through which each sign (as here, each word) is made up; the signi-fied is the lion and its name—the ideational content that is articulated by the units cut out by the signifiers: "because my name is lion." At the level of the individual sign the relation between signifier—letter—and signified—idea— and their conjunction would look like this: S^d/S^r = Sign.

But this sign, or string of signs, is found in a grammar book and thus "be-cause my name is lion" is not left at what could be called the denotational level where it is pointing to lions, to their habitats, to their strength, as in, let us say: "If I have taken the prey from my weaker fellow animals, it is, among other things, because my name is lion." Rather the Latin phrase is being used as an example, a mere instance of the grammatical agreement between subject and predicate. And as such an instance, the richness of the sign—the lion, its strength, its habitat, etc.—is itself divided from within. And a second layer, parasitical on the first meaning, is installed.

This second layer is formal; it is the subject/predicate structure of the sentence in which grammatical agreement is at stake—*any* instance of agreement, lions, snakes, butterflies, no matter. This formal layer constituting the phrase as "mere" example is thus empty. But it preys on the fullness of the layer of the sentence understood as meaning. And Barthes's argument is that for myth to work, it *must* prey on it.

So what is myth? Myth is depoliticized speech. Myth is ideology. Myth is the act of draining history out of signs and reconstructing these signs instead as "instances," in particular, instances of universal truths or of natural law, of things that have no history, no specific embeddedness, no territory of contestation. Myth steals into the heart of the sign to convert the historical into the "natural"—something that is uncontested, that is simply "the way things are." In the case of "because my name is lion," the myth is the combination of meaning and form into the content that reads: "this is the principle of agreement in Latin." But beyond that the mythical content conveys the importance of order and regularity in the structure of Latin, as well as one's sense, as reader, of belonging to a system of schooling in which many children like oneself are also learning this principle, and the idea that this principle is addressed to oneself, meant for oneself: "See! This is what 'grammatical agreement' looks like." This is what Barthes calls the *interpellant* aspect of mythical speech.[4] It is addressed to its readers, calling out to them, asking them to see and agree to the way this example confirms this principle, at one and the same time fading before the principle's authority—this is just an example—and filling that authority with a kind of subservient but needed specificity—see! nature is brimming with just the thing this means: "because my name is lion."

The more famous example Barthes uses in his analysis of mythical speech is one that is closer to Sherman's *Film Stills,* since it is not composed of letters and words but of a photograph and its depictions. It is a magazine cover of *Paris Match* in which a black soldier is shown giving the French salute. The photograph—as physical object, with its areas of dark and light—is the signifier; the depicted elements are the signified. They combine into the sign: a black soldier giving the French salute. That combination then becomes the support for the mythical content that is not just a message about French imperialism—"France is a global nation; there are black subjects who also serve it"—but a message about its *naturalness,* as the signified of the first order of the mythic support is called up as an example to fill up and instance its mythic contention: "Imperialism is not oppressive; it is natural, because we are all one humanity; you see! examples of how it works and the loyalty it engages can be found everywhere, anywhere, for example, in this photograph where a black soldier gives the French salute." The "you see!" part of the message is, of course, the interpellant part. It is the myth summoning its consumer to grasp the meaningfulness of the first order sign—the photograph-as-signified—and then to project his or her conviction in that unitary, simple meaning, onto the more complex, hazy, insinuating level of the contents of the myth.

So let's go back to Sherman and the *Rashomon*-factor: the critic sitting there in the darkened auditorium of the School of Visual Arts, looking at a set of slide comparisons and believing something about their replicative relationship, believing this to be the case because after all Sherman's work, he is certain, takes us back in any event to the real film we remember. What is crucial here is that he has bought the pitch and never thought to look under the hood. He has taken the first order sign as a composite, a signifier and signified already congealed into a finished meaning—actress X in film Y—and he has completed the mythical content. Here it would be something like: Cindy Sherman is an artist and artists imitate reality (Universal Truth No. 1), doing so through their own sensibilities, and thus adding something of themselves to it (Universal Truth No. 2). The formula we come out with was penned by Emile Zola. It goes: Art is important; it gives us a piece of nature seen through a temperament. Nature in the Sherman case would be of a somewhat technological kind, namely, the original film role, which Sherman would pass through the temperament of her own memory and projection; she would externalize this observed and felt bit of the world, and her work of art—the externalization of these emotions—will be her expression, with which we as viewers can empathize. Art = Emotion relayed through nature. That's the myth and that's why the critic has to produce—no matter through what process of self-deception or hallucination—the "original," the bit of nature, the filmic heroine in her role. That's what it's like to be a myth consumer. To buy the pitch. To fail to look under the hood.

What, then, is under the hood?

What is always under the hood is the signifier, the material whose very articulation conditions the signified. And further, working away under the hood, either *on* or *with* the signifier, is the effort perhaps to limit the possibility that it might produce a multiplicity of unstable signifieds and promote a sliding among them or, on the other hand, to do the reverse and welcome, even facilitate such sliding. Limitation is the work of realism in novels and films: to every signifier one and only one signified.[5] Conversely, sliding and proliferation has always interested the antirealist (what used to be called the *avant-garde*) artist.[6]

Work on the signifier is perfectly available for observation in Sherman's *Untitled Film Stills.* Take the group of images that includes *#21, #22,* and *#23.* In all three, Sherman wears the same costume, a dark, tailored suit with a white collar and a small straw cloche pulled onto a mop of short blond curls. But everything else changes from one still to the next: as in the first, *#21,* the register is close-up taken at a low angle; in the second, *#22,* a long shot intricates the character amid a complication of architectural detail and the cross fire of sun and shadow; and the last, *#23,* frames the figure in medium shot at the far right side of the image against the darkened emptiness of an undefined city street and flattened by the use of a wide-angle lens. And with each reframing and each new depth-of-field and each new condition of luminosity, "the character" transmogrifies, moving from type to type and from movie to movie. From *#21* and the Hitchcock heroine to *#23* and the hardened *film noir* dame, there is no "acting" involved.[7] Almost every single bit of the character—which is to say, of each of the three different characters—is a function of work on the signifier: the various things that in film go to make up a photographic style.

Untitled Film Still #21, 1978. Silver print, 8 x 10 inches.

Untitled Film Still #22, 1978. Silver print, 8 x 10 inches.

———

Untitled Film Still #23, 1978. Silver print, 8 x 10 inches.

It was just this that Judith Williamson, one of the early feminist writers on Sherman's work, described when she said that in the stills, "we are constantly forced to recognize a visual style (often you could name the director) simultaneously with a type of femininity. The two cannot be pulled apart. The image suggests that there is a particular kind of femininity in the *woman* we see, whereas in fact the femininity is in the image itself, it *is* the image."[8]

This fact that there is no free-standing character, so to speak, but only a concatenation of signifiers so that the persona is released—conceived, embodied, established—by the very act of cutting out the signifiers, making "her" a pure function of framing, lighting, distance, camera angle, and so forth, is what you find when you look under the hood. And Sherman as de-myth-ifier is specifically allowing us, encouraging us to look under the hood, even as she is also showing us the tremendous pull to buy into the myth—which is to say, to accept the signified as finished fact, as free-standing figure, as "character." Thus there is the tendency when speaking of the film stills to enumerate their personae, either as the roles—"a woman walking down a dark street at night; another, scantily clad, with martini in hand, peering out the sliding glass door of a cheap motel"[9]—or as the actresses who project them: Gina Lollabrigida, Monica Viti, Barbara Bel Geddes, Lana Turner . . .

That neither the roles nor the actresses are free-standing, that all are, within representation, effects—outcomes, functions—of the signifiers that body them forth is what Barthes labored to demonstrate in his extraordinary book *S/Z,* an analysis of the inner workings of literary realism. Showing that each "character" is produced through a concatenation of separate codes—some the signifiers or operators of difference, whether of gender (male/female) or age (young/old) or position (rich/poor); others the operators of references to general knowledge keyed into the text by the merest aside ("as in the Arabian Nights"); still others the operators of the puzzle that drives the narrative forward toward its Truth (who is? what is?)—what Barthes makes clear is that when a name finally arrives to refer to or denote a character, that name is buoyed up, carried along, by the underlying babble of the codes.[10] The name is thus the signified—

Untitled Film Still #7, 1978. Silver print, 8 x 10 inches.

the character—that the author slides onto the codes to produce realism's appear-ance that for every name there is a referent, a denotation, a unified empirical fact. What is being masked is that the name, rather than pointing to a primary entity in the "real," is an effect of the vast already-written, already-heard, already-read of the codes; it, the denotation, is merely the last of these codes to be slipped into place. The consumer of realist fiction, however, buys the pitch and believes in the "character," believes in the substance of the person from whom all the rest seems to follow as a set of necessary attributes, believes, that is, in the myth.

Most of those who write about the *Film Stills* acknowledge that Sherman is manipulating stereotypes and that though these are being relayed through a generalized matrix of filmic portrayals and projections, there is of course no real film, no "original," to which any one of them is actually referring. So the myth consumer of my opening anecdote is something of an exception and in that sense a straw man. And yet we have not far to look to find other versions of myth consumption, or the direct connection to the signified-as-instance.

One form of this that can be found in the mountainous literature on Sher-man's work is to assume that each of these signifieds is being offered as an in-stance of Sherman's own deeper self—the artist (as in Universal Truth No. 2, above) becoming the vehicle through which the fullness of humanity might be both projected and embraced in all its aspects. Peter Schjeldahl, for example, understands the individual *Film Still*'s signified to be Sherman's "fantasy of herself in a certain role, redolent usually of some movie memory," with all the different characters resonating together to form the totality of the artist's selfhood in her oracular role as "our" representative: "Sherman's special genius has been to locate the oracle not in the 'out there' of media bombardment but in the 'in here' of her own partly conditioned, partly original mind—a dense, rich sediment of half-remembered, half-dreamed image tones and fragments. . . . She has mined this sediment for ideas, creating an array of new, transpersonal images that spark across the gap between self and culture."[11] The mythic content Schjeldahl then consumes from these instances of the self-as-oracle is that it is in the nature of the artist to organize "messages that seem to tell us our nature and our fate."

Another form of myth consumption is to continue to buy into the finished signified of the role, the "character," but to see the multiplicity of these as various forms of what Arthur Danto seems to like to call The Girl. He provides his own roll call of these variants: The Girl in Trouble, The Girl Detective, The Girl We Left Behind, Daddy's Brave Girl, Somebody's Stenog, Girl Friday, The Girl Next Door, The Whore with the Golden Heart . . . But his point is that "The Girl is an allegory for something deeper and darker, in the mythic unconscious of everyone, regardless of sex. . . . Each of the stills is about The Girl in Trouble, but in the aggregate they touch the myth we each carry out of childhood, of danger, love and security that defines the human condition."[12] Although Danto turns here to the term *myth,* he uses it not in the manner of the de-myth-ifier, but as the unsuspicious myth consumer: buying into the signified of every variant of The Girl as an instance of the myth that there is a shared space of fantasy, or what he himself provides by way of mythic content as "the common cultural mind."

> . . . it is necessary to fly in the face of Sherman's own expressly non-, even anti-, theoretical stance.

> —*Laura Mulvey*[13]

Not surprisingly, given the fact that Sherman's *Film Stills* focus exclusively on women, on the roles women play in films, on the nature of those roles as preset, congealed, cultural clichés—hence their designation as "stereotype"— and by implication, on the pall that the real-world pressure to fill these roles casts over the fates of individual women, feminist writers have embraced Sherman's art, seeing it as "inseparable from the analyses—and the challenge—of feminist work on representation." But even as they have done so, they have been disgusted by its consumption as myth. For such consumption, they point out, inverts the terms of Sherman's work, taking the very thing she is holding up for critical inspection and transposing it into the grounds of praise.[14]

Arguing that there is, however, a logic—no matter how perverse—behind such a transposition, Abigail Solomon-Godeau sees a mechanism at work there to recut Sherman's art by exchanging what is dismissed as the narrow, somewhat threadbare cloth of feminist investigation for the more noble garments that drape the artist who addresses the humanity-in-general of "the common cultural mind." This, she reasons, is necessary to the art world's promotion of Sherman to the status of major artist, something incompatible with a feminist understanding of her enterprise. Therefore, as an apparatus of promotion (in both the media and museums) has supplanted other kinds of writing about Sherman, the mythical reading of the meaning of her work has followed. And thus it is no accident that Danto would need to recast the import of the *Film Stills* by insisting that they "are not in my view merely feminist parables." [15]

But it must be said that within feminism itself the import of the *Stills* has also been recast, a recasting that is articulated in Solomon-Godeau's essay, although buried in its footnotes. For if Judith Williamson's early treatment of the *Film Stills* appeared under the title "Images of Woman," Solomon-Godeau has now, eight years later, transposed this to "woman-as-image," and signaled to the reader the importance of this distinction. [16]

Indeed, almost two decades of work on the place of woman within representation has put this shift into effect, so that a whole domain of discourse no longer conceives of stereotype as a kind of mass-media mistake, a set of cheap costumes women might put on or cast-aside. Rather stereotype—itself rebaptized now as "masquerade," and here understood as a psychoanalytic term—is thought of as the phenomenon to which all women are submitted both inside and outside representation, so that as far as femininity goes, there is nothing *but* costume. Representation itself—films, advertisements, novels, and so forth— would thus be part of a far more absolute set of mechanisms by which characters are constructed: constructed equally in life as in film, or rather, equally in film because as in life. And in this logic woman is nothing but masquerade, nothing but image. As Laura Mulvey has described this shift: "The initial idea that images contributed to women's alienation from their bodies and from their sexuality, with an attendant hope of liberation and recuperation, gave way to theories of representation as symptom and signifier of the way problems posed by sexual difference under patriarchy could be displaced onto the feminine." [17]

It was Mulvey's own 1975 text, "Visual Pleasure and Narrative Cinema," that most formatively set out that latter argument in which woman is constructed as spectacle and symptom, becoming the passive object of a male gaze. Which is to say that in her essay a relation is set up among three terms: (1) the observation that there are gender distinctions between the roles that men and women play in films—males being the agents of the narrative's action; females being the passive objects or targets of that narrative, often interrupting the (masculine) action by the stasis of a moment of formal (feminine) opulence; (2) the conception that there is a gender assignment for the viewers of films, one that is unrelentingly male since the very situation of filmic viewing is structured as voyeuristic and fetishistic, its source of pleasure being essentially an eroticization of fetishism: "the determining male gaze projects its fantasy onto the female figure, which is styled accordingly," she writes; and (3) that these assignments of role are a function of the psychic underpinnings of all men and women, since they reflect the truths about the unconscious construction of gendered identity that psychoanalysis has brought to light: "Woman . . . stands in patriarchal culture as signifier for the male other, bound by a symbolic order in which man can live out his fantasies and obsessions through linguistic command, by imposing them on the silent image of woman still tied to her place as bearer of meaning, not maker of meaning."[18]

In that last sentence, which slides from the domain of filmic representations to the universal condition of how "woman stands in patriarchal culture," there are packed a large number of theoretical assumptions that knot together around concepts about the unconscious, castration, and the import of structural linguistics for psychoanalysis. Insofar as Sherman's work is implicated in those assumptions and the analysis about woman-as-image that flows from them—the *Film Stills,* for example, repeatedly presented as either a text to be explained by this analysis and/or a consequence of it—it is necessary to unpack these assumptions, no matter how schematically.

The psychic economy that drives men to activity and speech and women to passivity and silence is an economy that also separates looking from being looked at, spectator from spectacle. And that economy is organized, according to this reading of psychoanalysis, around castration anxiety, which is to say in terms of an event through which the child is made aware of sexual difference and, in one and the same moment, socialized by being subordinated to parental law. And if difference and the law converge in a single psychic configuration, they do so in relation to a visual event in which the possibility of absence is verified in the body of the "castrated" mother, the woman from whose genitals the phallus can be seen to be absent.[19] Siding with the paternal law, the child chooses speech, for which the master signifier is now the emblem of difference itself: the phallic signifier, the signifier as phallus.

It is in this sense that Mulvey refers to the male as maker of meaning in contrast to woman as bearer of meaning, a bearer now because the lack she is seen as manifesting on her own body, insofar as it sets up the phallus as signifier— which is to say a differential function through which the play of meaning now operates—this lack is necessary to the social system of order and sense to which Mulvey gives, following Jacques Lacan, the name Symbolic.[20] Thus she writes, "An idea of woman stands as linchpin to the system: it is her lack that produces the phallus as a symbolic presence, it is her desire to make good the lack that the phallus signifies."[21]

If the economy of sexual difference sets up a division of labor in relation to language, it also produces a separation of roles, it is argued, in relation to vision. On the one hand cinematic pleasure is scopophilic, voyeuristic: it wants to see and to control its objects of sight—but at a distance, protected by its own remove in the dark and at a point of vantage that perspective triangulates for it, the occupant of this point guaranteed, through this visually unified position of control, a sense of its own (phallic) mastery. On the other hand this pleasure is put in jeopardy by the very image of the woman it wishes to master insofar as that woman is marked as well as the bearer of the threat of castration. Thus it is necessary for this spectator to convoke the psychic mechanism of denial, for which the classic psychoanalytic instance is fetishism: the male child entering a perversion in which he sees the proof of sexual difference but continues none-theless to believe in the woman as "whole," not-castrated: the phallic mother.

The fetish constructed through this mechanism of denial thus restores to her body what is known to be "missing."

If film works constantly to re-create woman as a symptom of man's castration anxiety—thus silencing her—it also works, and here even harder, to situate her as eroticized fetish: the image of lack papered over, the emblem of wholeness restored. Woman is in this sense skewered in place as an image that simultaneously establishes her as other than man—the Truth that it is he who possesses the phallus—and at the same time the fetishized image of the whole body from which nothing is missing.

Stephen Heath describes this visual scenario from the point of view of the gazing male subject—"Everything turns on the castration complex and the central phallus, its visibility and the spectacle of lack; the subject, as Lacan puts it at one point, 'looks at itself in its sexual member'"—and then for the consequences for the woman secured as spectacle:

> What the voyeur seeks, poses, is not the phallus on the body of the other but its absence as the definition of the mastering presence, the security, of his position, his seeing, his phallus; the desire is for the other to be spectacle not subject, or only the subject of that same desire, its exact echo. . . . Fetishism too, which often involves the scopophilic drive, has its scenario of the spectacle of castration; and where what is at stake is not to assert that the woman has the penis-phallus but to believe in the intact, to hold that the woman is not castrated, that nothing is lost, that his representation, and of him, works. Always, from voyeurism to fetishism, the eroticization of castration.[22]

It is with this theoretical armature in place, then, that Laura Mulvey herself looks at the *Film Stills,* understanding them to be rehearsing this structure of the male gaze, of the voyeurist constructing the woman in endless repetitions of her vulnerability and his control: "The camera looks; it 'captures' the female character in a parody of different voyeurisms. It intrudes into moments in which she is unguarded, sometimes undressed, absorbed into her own world in the privacy of her own environment. Or it witnesses a moment in which her guard drops as she is suddenly startled by a presence, unseen and off-screen, watching her."[23]

And yet, we could say, it is this very theoretical armature that operates in such a description to put a mythic reading of the *Film Stills* in place, one that is not taking the trouble, indeed, to look under the hood. Judith Williamson had seen the constructed role emerge in the *Stills* as a consequence of the signifiers through which any filmic image must be built—"the two cannot be pulled apart," she had said; Laura Mulvey, on the other hand, is buying into a signified-as-instance, a congealed sign, the semantic totality that reads "woman-as-image," or again, "woman as object of the male gaze."

Sherman, of course, has a whole repertory of women being watched and of the camera's concomitant construction of the watcher for whom it is proxy. From the very outset of her project, in *Untitled Film Still #2* (1977), she sets up the sign of the unseen intruder. A young girl draped in a towel stands before her bathroom mirror, touching her shoulder and following her own gesture in its reflected image. A doorjamb to the left of the frame places the "viewer" outside this room. But what is far more significant is that this viewer is constructed as a hidden watcher by means of the signifier that reads as graininess, a diffusion of the image that constructs the signified /distance/, a severing of the psychic space of the watcher from that of the watched. In *Untitled Film Still #39* (1979), it is not so much the grain of the emulsion that establishes the voyeuristic remove, with its sense that one is stealing up on the woman, as it is a kind of nimbus that washes around the frame of the image, repeating in the register of light the sense of barrier that the door frame constructs in the world of physical objects.

But in *Untitled Film Still #81* (1979) there is a remarkably sharp depth of field, so that such /distance/ is gone, despite the fact that doorways are once again an obtrusive part of the image, implying that the viewer is gazing at the woman from outside the space she physically occupies. As in the other cases, the

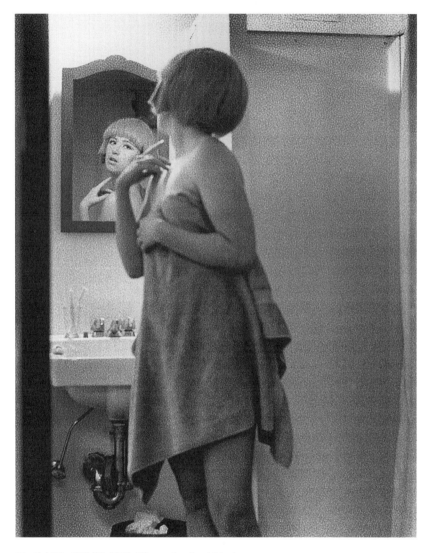

Untitled Film Still #2, 1978. Silver print, 8 x 10 inches.

Untitled Film Still #39, 1979. Silver print, 8 x 10 inches.

Untitled Film Still #81, 1979. Silver print, 8 x 10 inches.

woman appears to be in a bathroom and once again she is scantily dressed, wearing only a thin nightgown. Yet the continuity established by the focal length of the lens creates an unimpeachable sense that her look at herself in the mirror reaches past her reflection to include the viewer as well. Which is to say that as opposed to the idea of /distance/, there is here the signified /connection/, and what is further cut out as the signified at the level of narrative is a woman chatting to someone (perhaps another woman) in the room outside her bathroom as she is preparing for bed.

The narrative impact of these images tends to submerge the elements through which it is constructed, elements such as depth-of-field, grain, light, etc. which, it would seem, are too easy to dismiss as merely "formal" integers, whereas they function as signifiers crucial to the semantic effect. That Sherman is concentrated on these aspects is made very palpable in the one *Film Still* that seems inexplicable within the series as a whole: *#36* (1979). Of all the *Stills* this one is so severely backlit that nothing can be seen of the character's face and almost nothing of her body beyond its silhouette. Standing in front of a curtain through which the powerful backlighting is dramatically diffused, she extends one of her arms upward almost out of frame; the other bends to grasp the elbow of the first in what could be a gesture of washing but remains radically ambiguous. As pattern her body reads black on the white of the ground, and her garments—the bodice of her slip and the stiffened film of a crinoline—parted slightly from her body, create the only area of modulation or middle tone in the image. To a far greater degree than almost any other in the series, this work is deprived of narrative implication.

A few months prior to the making of this *Still,* an image—or rather two images—remarkably like it were published: two photographs by Edgar Degas, of a ballerina dressed in a low-cut bodice, her skirt a diaphanous crinoline, standing in front of a luminous curtain and reaching with one arm upward, her other arm bent inward at the elbow. These photographs, published by a critic who just a few months later would launch Sherman in an essay called "Pictures," an article providing the first serious critical context for her work (Sherman's first solo

Untitled Film Still #36, 1979. Silver print, 8 x 10 inches.

exhibition was still one year away), are related to one another through an extraordinary ambiguity with regard to light.[24] For having solarized the negative of his photograph to create reversals between negative and positive areas within the image, Degas then created both a negative and a positive print. And the dark/light reversals that arise from this treatment constitute the dancer as a phantom whose existence can be located nowhere. As Douglas Crimp described it:

> In the print in which the right arm and torso of the dancer appears
> to be normally positive, the shadow of the arm on the wall she grasps
> appears as a streak of light. Her face, also apparently in shadow, and
> her "dark" hair are registered as light. At this point, obviously, lan-
> guage begins to fail. How can we any longer speak of light and dark?
> How can we speak of a white shadow? a dark highlight? a translucent
> shoulder blade? When light and dark, transparency and opacity, are
> reversed, when negative becomes positive and positive, negative, the
> referents of our descriptive language are dissolved. We are left with
> a language germane only to the photographic, in which the manipu-
> lation of light generates its own, exclusive logic.[25]

And in the publication of the twinned Degas photographs, the same dancer turns to confront her own mirror image as, flipped from negative to positive, she is also flipped left and right. Folded in a way almost impossible to imagine around the axis of her own body, that body is folded as well around a ghostly condition of luminosity that produces it now as solid, now as if in X-ray.

Sherman's *Untitled Film Still #36,* in its condition of being *hors série,* has also the aura of this impossibly folded Degas dancer, turning in a light that has no focus, and indeed no possible external point of view. Perhaps the *Still* was addressed, imaginatively, to Crimp; but such an address has nothing in it of the theorization of the male gaze and the psycho-politics of sadistic control. Further, as we will see, this kind of backlighting, and all that it does to fragment the gaze, will emerge as a crucial element—or signifier—in Sherman's work of the early 1980s. But that is to anticipate somewhat, getting ahead of our story.

The Horizontals

The only thing cinemascope is good for is to film snakes and funerals.

—*Jean-Luc Godard*[26]

The *Film Stills* had been a laboratory for exploring the range of signifiers that go together to produce the look of a given filmic genre or director and thereby to construct a "character," sealing it as the "real" of denotation, which in Barthes's terms, as we've seen, is only the last of the cinematic, connotational codes to be slipped into place. It was from this various testing ground that Sherman then began to select out a single signifier, so as to concentrate on it.

First, in 1980, this signifier was the special effect of backscreen projection with its resultant fissure in the image field, the split it sets up in the experience of density and substance between the three-dimensional character and her flattened, fictitious-looking scenic surrounds. Color, which entered Sherman's work at this moment, heightened the sense of this difference.

Then, in 1981, a different signifier, put in place in the series triggered by a commission for a centerfold for *Artforum* magazine, emerged as the central concern. That signifier is point of view. And in this group of images that viewpoint, consistent through most of the series and stridently adopted by the camera, is from above, looking down. It is as though the extreme horizontality of the image's format had suggested a corresponding horizontality in the image field. From being a projection of the viewer looking outward toward a visual field imagined as parallel to the vertical of the upright body of the beholder and his or her plane of vision, the view now slides floorward to declare the field of vision itself as horizontal.

But if this in fact has happened, it has never been registered in the writing that greeted this phase of Sherman's work. Still firmly fixed on the signified, the projected roles—"In several of these, a girl is seen in a state of revery, day-dreaming—we automatically presume since we subliminally recall so many

Untitled #93, 1981. Color photograph, 24 x 48 inches.

scenes like these from movies and television—about her prospects for romance"[27]—the accounts of the series go straight for the mythic content: Sherman's ability to get inside her characters. "What is instantly recognizable in Sherman's new pictures is the universal state of daydream or reverie, the moments of harmless, necessary psychosis that are a recurring mechanism in anyone's mental economy. These are moments when consciousness dissolves back into itself, when wish and reality, personal and collective memory are one and the physical world ceases to exist."[28]

Mulvey, also, focuses on the characters and their interiors: "The young women that Sherman impersonates may be daydreaming about a future romance, or they may be mourning a lost one. They may be waiting, in enforced passivity, for a letter or telephone call. Their eyes gaze into the distance. They are not aware of their clothes, which are sometimes carelessly rumpled, so that, safe alone with their thoughts, their bodies are, slightly, revealed to the viewer." Referring to this effect as "soft-core pastiche" and associating the horizontal format of the images to the shape of a cinemascope screen, Mulvey's reading returns to the woman-as-image question, the construction of the eroticized fetish. "These photographs reiterate the 'to-be-looked-at-ness' of femininity," she writes, pointing to the way the connotations of intimacy both at the level emotion—daydream, fantasy—and of setting—the bedroom—combine to exude a strong sense of sexuality. And even though the voyeuristic place of the spectator is not marked here, as it has been in the *Film Stills,* she says, the issue of woman-as-spectacle, woman-as-symptom has not changed. It has merely been reconditioned to concentrate on the mechanism of masquerade: the posturing projected outward from an empty center. It is in this series, she writes, that the works "start to suggest an interior space, and initiate [Sherman's] exploration inside the masquerade of femininity's interior/exterior binary opposition."[29]

It was in his essay "The Meaning of the Phallus" that Jacques Lacan had formulated masquerade as this desperate binary, pronouncing: "Paradoxical as this formulation might seem, I would say that it is in order to be the phallus, that is to say, the signifier of the desire of the Other, that a woman will reject an essential part of femininity, namely all its attributes via masquerade."[30] Thus, if femininity is unconsciously constructed—insofar as it is projected as lack, as what is missing, and in this sense as symptom of the man—as an essential absence, Lacan describes the woman as rejecting that absence, and thus her own "essence," in order to assume the masquerade of wholeness, of the nothing-missing of the fetish. The dance of her "to-be-looked-at-ness" is a veil covering over this nothing, which Lacan elsewhere designates as "not-all"—*pas-tout*.

It is in this same text that Lacan had cautioned that the phallus in being a signifier could not be seen as either a phantasmatic object or a physical organ: "Nor is it as such an object (part, internal, good, bad, etc. . . .) in so far as this term tends to accentuate the reality involved in a relationship. It is even less the organ, penis or clitoris, which it symbolizes."[31] Instead, as signifier it opposes the signified, and—as in the relationship described by structural linguistics—it "has an active function in determining the effects in which the signifiable appears as submitting to its mark, becoming through that passion the signified."

It is, of course, the human subject who in this sense emerges as "submitting to its mark," emerging as the material through which language itself speaks, "his nature woven by effects in which we can find the structure of language." Spoken thus by this chain of signifiers that operate to cut him out as their effect, their signified, the human subject is, then, the subject of this system. In another essay Lacan formulated the rule of this linguistic subject as $\forall \chi \, \Phi \chi$, which reads *all x is a function of the phallus,* with phallus understood here as the master signifier in the linguistic chain.[32] It is a formulation that announces once again the sense in which the human subject is not its own master but is organized elsewhere, in the place Lacan designates as Other and is occupied by the unconscious, by language, by social law.

But it is also the case that every human subject has an ego, or sense of (autonomous) self, that wants to hold out against that formula and would instead organize itself in other, directly opposing terms: $\exists \chi \, \overline{\phi \chi}$, which reads *there is an x that is not a function of the phallus.* This protest is an insistance that there is something that "I really am"—"beneath my surfaces and roles and socializations, beyond my sex and my childhood, away from everything that conspires to keep me from saying what" it is.[33] For Stephen Melville, writing on Lacanian notions of the subject, the combination (or rather the togetherness-in-opposition) of these two formulations "seems to capture something of the primordial and constitutive alienation that Lacan takes to characterize human being."

Now if the ego can insist that "there is an *x*—me!—that is not a function of the phallus," it is because, Lacan argues, that ego has first constituted itself in relation to an image of wholeness, a unitary figure or gestalt, that it has seen in a mirror. And that ego will continue to find instances of wholeness with which to reconstitute the "there is . . ." throughout its existence, one example of which is, of course, the setting up of the woman as fetish, as *pas-tout*. In a certain way this securing of the ego in relation to the instance takes a form that is very like what Barthes had called the interpellant function of myth, the "you see! here is . . ." Which is to say that if the subject is no longer the *source* of his own meanings in the field of the symbolic (the chain of signifiers), the very production of meaning out there in the field of representation will itself project an image of wholeness (the sign as unit) that will be mirrored back to him as an interpellant fiction. And this will set him up as the unified, although imaginary, recipient of the "you see! . . ."

Now, if I have been rehearsing these theories, so central for the feminist theorization of woman-as-image, it is in order to get a sense of what the mechanisms are that prevent a critic like Mulvey from looking under the hood. It is to be able to speculate on why a certain meaning of Sherman's "horizontals" would have remained invisible, namely, the one marked /horizontal/.

Yet all we have to do is to focus on the insistent verticalization inscribed by all the metaphors that circulate through the Lacanian universe of the subject—the vertical of the mirror, the vertical of the veil, the vertical of the phallus as instance of wholeness, the vertical of the field of the fetish, the vertical of the plane of beauty—to sense why the horizontal is forced to recede from view when one's eyes are fixed on this theory.

Wherever Sherman's eyes are in relation to this or any theory, they are certainly attuned to the givens of her own field of operations, which is to say both high art and mass media. And in that field vertical and horizontal are exceedingly overdetermined. If the vertical is the axis of painting, the axis in which the picture orients itself to the wall, it is also, as we have seen, the axis of the plane of vision. That plane, which the Gestalt psychologists characterize as insistently "fronto-parallel" to the upright body of the viewer, is as well, they tell us, the plane of *Prägnanz,* by which they mean the hanging together or coherence of form. Thus the very drive of vision to formulate form, to project coherence in a mirroring of the body's own shape, will already mark even the empty vertical plane as a reflection of that body, heavier at the bottom, lighter at the top, and with a different orientation from right side to left. And conversely any location of form—of shape or of figure—will assume its place in an axis that is imaginatively vertical, even if we confront it on the page of the magazine we hold on our laps or in the tiles of the mosaic that lies under our feet.

Further, this vertical dimension, in being the axis of form, is also the axis of beauty. That is what Freud adds to the Gestaltists' picture: in that period in his evolution when man finally stood up, he left the world of sniffing and pawing, with nose pressed to genitals, and entered the world of vision in which objects were now experienced as being at a distance. And in this distancing his carnal instincts were *sublimated,* Freud writes, reorganized away from the organ world of the horizontal and into the formal world of the vertical, which is to say, of the beautiful.[34]

It was not just modernist painting, which formed part of Sherman's heritage as an artist, that insisted on this verticality—and its effect of sublimation; it was also the media universe of movies and television and advertising that declared it. And these two fields, so seemingly inimical to one another, had a bizarrely complementary relation to this effect of sublimation. If the media's fetish occupied the axis of the vertical, that very axis had itself become the fetish of high art.

During the 1960s and 1970s, however, a series of blows had been struck against this fetish. There were, to take only one example, a group of readings of the work of Jackson Pollock—itself a dominant emblem of the sublimatory condition of the vertical, optically conditioned, pictorial field—that defiantly reinterpreted Pollock's painting as horizontal. This was true of Andy Warhol's *Oxidation* paintings through which he read Pollock's dripped pictures as the work of a urinary trace (as though made by a man standing over a supine field and peeing), thus insisting on the way Pollock's canvases are permanently marked by the horizontality of their making. It was also true of Robert Morris's felts and scatter pieces, through which he reinterpreted Pollock's enterprise as "anti-form," by which he meant its condition of having yielded to gravity in assuming the axis of the horizontal. It can also be said that it was true of Ed Ruscha's *Liquid Word* pictures, with their reading of the significance of the drip technique as opening onto the dimension of entropy and "base materialism."[35]

If this sequence is invoked here it is to give one a sense of the connotations of the /horizontal/ within the field of the avant-garde of the 1960s and 1970s as certain artists opposed the /vertical/ within which is inscribed all forms of sublimation, whether that be of *the beautiful* or of *the fetish*. It is to see the work already in place on the pictorial signifier once it operates in terms of the failure to resist the pull of gravity, of the pivoting out of the axis of form.

In the "horizontals" Sherman's work is joined to this tradition. That de-sublimation is part of what she is encoding by means of the /horizontal/ will become unmistakably clear by the end of the 1980s with what are sometimes politely referred to as the "bulemia" pictures, namely, images in which the horizontal plane occupied by the point of view is forcibly associated with vomit, mold, and all forms of the excremental—"base materialism," indeed. But in these works of 1981 it is already clear that the view downward is desublimatory. In *Untitled #92* the narrative operated by this signifier is not that of "vulnerability" via a pose that is "soft and limp," but rather of animality, the body clenched in a kind of subhuman fixation. And in *Untitled #91* the network of cast shadows that grids the body and face of the woman projects over the image a sense of decay and of death. It is as though something were working against the forces of form and of life, attacking them, dissolving them, disseminating them into the field of the horizontal.

The theory of the male gaze, even as it moves from an analysis of the operations of a representational field—movies, paintings—to a generalization about the structure of human consciousness, has had to blind itself to its own fetishization of the vertical. Which is to say that it has had to blind itself to any-

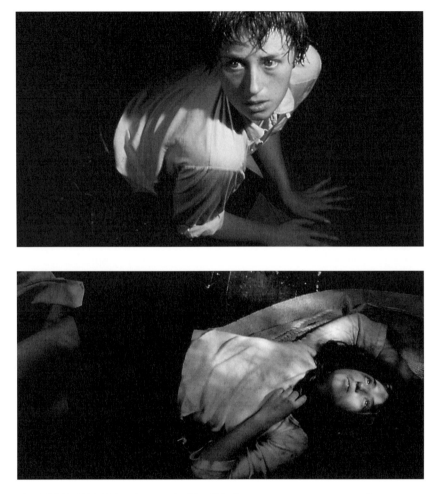

Untitled #92, 1981. Color photograph, 24 x 48 inches.

Untitled #91, 1981. Color photograph, 24 x 48 inches.

thing outside the vertical register of the image/form.[36] It is because of this that the theorists of the gaze repeat, at the level of analysis, the very fixity they are describing as operating the male gaze at the level of its social effects. And the symptom of this repetition is the constant submission to the meaning-effect the system generates, a submission to be found in Mulvey's steady consumption of Sherman's work as myth.

GLEAMS AND REFLECTIONS

> In short, the point of gaze always participates in the ambiguity of the jewel.
>
> —*Jacques Lacan*[37]

In the view of its theorists, the male gaze can do its work of continually putting the fetish/form in place even in the absence of any identifiable image. Victor Burgin, for example, argues that the effect of the gestalt's delineation and boundary can be generated by the very surfaces of media artifacts, such as the glossiness of the photographic print, with its high resolution and its glazed finish.

And Mulvey follows Burgin in this argument. For even while she reads the "horizontals" in terms of "the 'to-be-looked-at-ness' of femininity," she also admits that there is a contradiction between the limpness she sees in the poses—"polar opposites of a popular idea of fetishized femininity (high-heeled and corseted erect, flamboyant and exhibitionist)"—as well as the limpness of the image—"Sherman's use of color and of light and shade merges the female figure and her surroundings into a continuum, without hard edges"—and the sharp definition characteristic of the fetish. But fetishism, she argues, "returns in the formal qualities of the photography. The sense of surface now resides, not in the female figure's attempt to save her face in a masquerade of femininity, but in the model's subordination to, and imbrication with, the texture of the photographic medium itself."[38]

This texture, "in keeping," as Mulvey writes, "with the codes and conventions of commercial photography," is glossiness, the product of a kind of reflective veneer. It is this shiny surface that Burgin in his turn had related to the fetishized *glanz,* or gleam, that Freud had described in his essay outlining the unconscious mechanics of the construction of the fetish.[39]

Now while it is true that shininess functions as a certain kind of support for media images—and not just those of photography but even more insistently of backlit advertising panels and film and television screens—it is also true that Sherman performs specific work on this phenomenon. Just as she had taken a horizontal format—borrowed both from centerfold photographs and from cinemascope screens—and worked on it to produce a signifier that (in opposition to the meaning of the /vertical/) would cut out a specific signified—the /horizontal-as-lowness, -as-baseness/—so, here as well, the gleam is submitted to sustained investigation.

One of the last of the horizontals, *Untitled #95,* had announced this attention to the gleam. It is of a woman sitting upright on a bed (and thus no longer aligned with the horizontal axis of the format), caught in a strong glow of backlighting, so that her hair, now reconfigured as an intensely luminous nimbus, displaces the focus away from her face. As Sherman's work advances into the 1980s it repeats this kind of backlighting, forcing a glow to emerge from the ground of the image to advance outward at the viewer and thus to disrupt conditions of viewing, producing the figure herself as a kind of blind spot. We find it again, for example, in *Untitled #139* (1984).

But although backlighting is a very direct signifier for this sense of a diffracted and dispersed visual field, it is not the only means to produce it. Indeed it could be said that a certain effect of "wild light," the scattering of gleams around the otherwise darkened image as though refracting it through the facets of an elaborate jewel, will also create this corrosive visual dispersal. An early example of such wild light immediately followed the last of the horizontals, in *Untitled #110* (1982), where Sherman has concentrated on creating a sense of the completely aleatory quality of the illumination. For while the lighting plunges three quarters of the field into total blackness, it picks out the arm and

Untitled #95, 1981. Color photograph, 28 x 48 inches.

Untitled #110, 1982. Color photograph, 45 1/2 x 30 inches.

draped edge of the figure's garment to create a glowing, knotted complex of near unintelligibility.

Another instance of wild light is *Untitled #147* (1985), where head and upper torso given in enormous close-up are plunged into a darkness only violated by the backlit fragments of a bit of hair and one shoulder, and—building the eerie significance of the work—the reflected gleam of a pupil that emerges from the obscurity of the rest of the face like an utterly opaque, black marble.[40] This contrast between the opacity of the figure's look and the quality of light beaming outward at the viewer from dispersed parts of the rest of the image sets up a condition that can be generalized to other parts of this series I am calling Gleams and Reflections. It is a condition that I would like, now in my own turn, to use the work of Lacan to illuminate; although unlike the theory of the male gaze, this condition of the uncanny gaze, which Lacan qualifies as "the gaze as *objet a*," works against the effects of sublimation.

In setting up the model of this gaze as *objet a,* Lacan specifically contrasts it to the ego-model, itself linked to the vantage point of the perspective diagram, through which the "it's me!" of the subject, escaping from the dispersed condition of the Symbolic (the chain of signifiers) into the unified gestalt of the Imaginary, projects itself as whole. This projection, as we remember, is used in the male gaze theory to link the institution of the fetish to the very conditions of vision, understood as mapped by perspective's optical pyramid.

In the four lectures devoted to the question of the gaze, Lacan, however, is intent on restricting this optico-visual model, which he terms "geometral," to the realm of an idealized, abstracted, Cartesian conception of space. In the place of this spatial conception, he wishes to set a more fundamental condition of visuality, namely, that of light. Contrasting this luminous surround to the model of linear perspective, he says that we encounter the visual "not in the straight line, but in the point of light—the point of irradiation, the play of light, fire, the source from which reflections pour forth."[41]

Such an irradiation beaming at the subject from everywhere in space, bathing and surrounding him or her, cannot, then, be assimilated to the mirror image in which a gaze looks back at the subject in an imitation of the single

Untitled #147, 1985. Color photograph, 49 1/2 x 72 1/2 inches.

point from which the subject sees himself seeing. Instead, to depict this luminous gaze, which makes of the subject a *speculum mundi,* Lacan turns to the model of animal mimicry, which his old friend Roger Caillois had described back in the 1930s as the effect of space at large on a subject (-insect) who, yielding to the force of this space's generalized gaze, loses its own organic boundaries and merges with its surrounds in an almost psychotic act of imitation.[42] Making itself into a kind of shapeless camouflage, this mimetic subject now becomes a part of the "picture" of space in general: "It becomes a stain, it becomes a picture, it is inscribed in the picture," Lacan insists.[43] But if Caillois had been describing animal behavior, Lacan elaborates this effect for the human subject as well. Telling an anecdote about himself caught in an indefinable beam of light reflected off a sardine can, Lacan draws the conclusion:

> I am taking the structure at the level of the subject here, and it reflects something that is already to be found in the natural relation that the eye inscribes with regard to light. I am not simply that punctiform being located at the geometral point from which the perspective is grasped. No doubt, in the depths of my eye, the picture is painted. The picture, certainly, is in my eye. But I, I am in the picture.[44]

The sliding back and forth between Caillois's insect and Lacan's "I" in this discussion of mimicry is important to what Lacan wants to get at by this notion of gaze. For Caillois had insisted that the insect cannot be shown to assume its camouflage for purposes of adaptation—and thus what could be seen as coming from an intentional, subjective ground (no matter how instinctual or unconscious)—but simply as matter flowing into other matter, a mere body yielding to the call of space. Lacan joins this same position when he says, "Mimicry reveals something insofar as it is distinct from what might be called an *itself* that is behind," which is to say, distinct from a subjective ground of the subject.[45] Rather, we pass into the "picture" as mere "stain," which is to say as physical matter, as body. And here Lacan also refers to Merleau-Ponty's position in *The Phenomenology of Perception* that our relation to space—insofar as it is the target of the gaze constituted by the luminous surround, a light that catches us in its beam from behind as well as from in front—founds our perception not in the transparency of a conceptual grasp of space (as in the "geometral") but in the thickness and density of the body that simply intercepts the light.[46]

It is in this sense that to be "in the picture" is not to feel interpellated by society's *meaning*—"it's me!"—is not to feel, that is, whole; it is to feel dispersed, subject to a picture organized not by form but by formlessness. The desire awakened by the impossibility of occupying all those multiple points of the luminous projection of the gaze is a desire that founds the subject in the realization of a point of view that is withheld, one(s) that he or she cannot occupy. And it is the very fragmentation of that "point" of view that prevents this invisible, unlocatable gaze from being the site of coherence, meaning, unity, gestalt, *eidos*. Desire is thus not mapped here as the desire for form, and thus for sublimation (the vertical, the gestalt, the law); desire is modeled in terms of a transgression against form. It is the force invested in desublimation.[47]

Nowhere is the notion of having become "the picture" more searingly evoked than in Sherman's *Untitled #167* (1986), where the camouflage effect is in full flower. The figure, now absorbed and dispersed within the background, can only be picked out by a few remnants still visible, though only barely, in the mottled surface of the darkened detritus that fills the image. We make out the tip of a nose, the emergence of a finger with painted nail, the detached grimace of a set of teeth. Horizontalized, the view downward mapped by the image puts the signifier of the dissolution of the gestalt in place. But as it reaches the bottom edge of the image, the spectator's view encounters a gaze that projects toward it from within this matrix of near-invisibility. Reflected in the tiny mirror of a discarded compact, this gaze cannot be identified with any source in the image. Instead it seems to join all the other gleams and reflected points of light in the image to constellate the signifier for the /unlocatable/, and thus for the transgression of the gestalt.

Untitled #167, 1987. Color photograph, 61 1/2 x 91 1/8 inches.

Throughout the late 1980s Sherman continued to figure this field of the unlocatable gaze by means of Gleams and Reflections. And now the bouncing light of these opaquely slippery, arborescent signifiers is more consistently married to the /horizontal/, both combining in a drive toward the desublimation of the image. In *Untitled #168* (1987) a glowing but imageless television screen joins the repertory of gleams. In *Untitled #176* (1987) the refractive surface of water sparkling upward to meet the downwardly focused view of the spectator, projects the multiple points of light with all the ambiguity of the jewel that produces not the beautiful of sublimation but the formless pulsation of desire.

THE OLD MASTERS

The core of [Leonardo's] nature, and the secret of it, would appear to be that after his curiosity had been activated in infancy in the service of sexual interests he succeeded in sublimating the greater part of his libido into an urge for research.

—*Sigmund Freud*[48]

In his *Three Essays on the Theory of Sexuality* Freud speaks of the sexual instincts of children as relentlessly and repetitively driving them toward what they want to know but dare not ask, and what they want to see but dare not uncover behind the garments that conceal it. This drive, which is sexual, does not cause pleasure for the child, but to the contrary, nonpleasure "in view of the direction of the subject's development." Therefore to ward off this nonpleasure, a defense against the drive sets in, in the form of disgust, shame, and morality. This defense Freud calls reaction-formation.

But parallel to this is another defense against the force of the drive, namely, that of sublimation. This occurs when the drive is forced to change its course by shifting its object. Thus the sexual instinct can be "diverted ('sublimated') in the direction of art, if its interest can be shifted away from the genitals on to the shape of the body as a whole." This shift is, as we know, away from the libidinal and on to the beautiful of form.[49]

In 1989 and 1990 Sherman turned her own attention to Art, which is to say, firmly and steadily toward the most overt and pronounced version of the scene of sublimation. The very term *high* that modifies *art* (either explicitly or implicitly) announces this sublimatory effect as having had its origin in a gesture of raising one's eyes to the plane of the vertical and of thereby acceding to the field of the gestalt. And Sherman's "Old Master" pictures revel in forming again and again the signifiers of the form that high art celebrates, signifiers of verticality meshing with signifiers of the unitariness of the gestalt.

Premiere among these, of course, is the signifier constellated by the frame. For the frame is what produces the boundary of the work of art as something secreted away from ordinary space-at-large, thereby securing the work of art's autonomy; and at the same time the frame's contour echoes the conditions of boundary and closure that are the very foundations of form.

Sometimes the frame enters the field of the aesthetic image through nothing more complex than the black background that cushions and cradles the figure, emphasizing its shape by contrast, a shape that in its turn is often constructed as a set of miniaturized echoes of the larger, enclosing frame. These internalized echoes might appear in the encircling oval formed by the figure's arms, meeting in a gesture of self-embrace. Or they may be the result of the U of a bodice that frames the head and upper torso, or the encircling O of a turban that frames the face. Sometimes the frame is projected by more scenographic elements: painted curtains that part to make a space for the figure; or even the depiction of an actual frame behind the figure—the ornate frame of a mirror, perhaps, in which the figure can now be doubly enfolded, first by the actual frame of the painting as a whole, and second by the depicted frame that captures and embraces the figure's double.

Two of the very famous Old Master images that Sherman stages represent the extremes of these possibilities, from most simple to most elaborate. Her version of *La Fornarina,* the portrait of Raphael's mistress (*Untitled #205* [1989]),

Untitled #221, 1990. Color photograph, 48 x 30 inches.

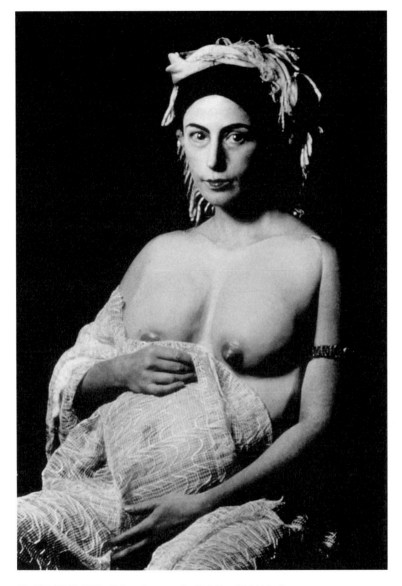

Untitled #205, 1989. Color photograph, 61 1/2 x 48 1/4 inches.

Untitled #204, 1989. Color photograph, 67 3/4 x 57 1/4 inches.

presents us with the first alternative, while her strangely composite projection of several of Ingres's most celebrated sitters—Madame Rivière, Madame de Senonines, and Madame Moitessier (*Untitled #204* [1989])—confronts us with the second. In this last the signifiers of internal framing are piled one upon the other as drapery, gesture, and mirror encircle the projected body in a giddy enactment of frames-within-frames.

Further, another rather disturbing signifier enters this theater of the /vertical/ to point to still one more meaning of *high* in the conception of high art. This signifier, a function of the way these Old Master personages are constructed by Sherman thanks to fake body parts that are strapped onto her torso or applied to her head, marks the surface of the image as a mask or veil, one that can supposedly be removed, pushed aside, seen behind. In their very detachability, these elements point thus to the hermeneutic dimension of the work of art: the idea that it possesses an inner truth or meaning to which the interpreter might penetrate. In being a hermeneutic object the work of art thus occupies the "high" position not as vertical to horizontal but as ideal to material, or as mind to body.

And yet it is also in the obviousness of the condition of these body parts as prostheses that they work against the conception of the veil with its hidden Truth, at the very same time that they burrow into the /vertical/ to oppose and topple it. Conniving against the sublimatory energy of Art, the body parts constitute signifiers that mark a yield to gravity, both because of the weight of the physical elements they model, and the sense they promote of these pendulous forms already sliding down the surface of the body. In this capacity they elaborate the field of a desublimatory, horizontal axis that erodes the facade of the vertical, bearing witness to the fact that behind that facade there lies not the transparency of Truth, of meaning, but the opacity of the body's matter, which is to say, the formless.

It is as though Sherman's own earlier work with the /horizontal/ has now led her back to the vertical, sublimated image, but only to disbelieve it. Greeting the vertical axis with total skepticism, the Old Master images work to discorroborate it, to deflate it, to stand in the way of its interpellant effect.

THE VOMIT PICTURES

> However, even this bedrock—the vomit and the blood for in-
> stance—returns to cultural significance: that is, to the difficulty of
> the body, and above all the female body, while it is subjected to the
> icons and narratives of fetishism.
>
> —*Laura Mulvey*[50]

Nothing, it would seem, could be less alike than Sherman's impersonation of various Raphaels and Davids and Ingres and the series she worked on over roughly the same time period (1987–91), to which various descriptive rubrics have been given, among them "bulimia" and "vomit." And yet the notion of the veil can operate for both series: either in the manner of a hermeneutics of the work of art, as described above; or, for the bulimia pictures, in the manner of what Mulvey has called the "phantasmagoria of the female body."

Indeed, as has often been pointed out, the female body itself has been made to serve as a metaphor for hermeneutics, which is to say as the Truth to which one might penetrate upon lifting the veil of the work. But Mulvey's "phantasmagoria" recasts this Truth into its psychoanalytic dimension and shows it as yet one more avatar of fetishism. For the truth that was sought behind the veil, the truth for which the woman-as-fetish now functions as symptom, is the truth of the wound inflicted by a phantasmatic castration. Thus the interior of the female body is projected as a kind of lining of bodily disgust—of blood, of excreta, of mucous membranes. If the woman-as-fetish/image is the cosmetic facade erected against this wound, the imagined penetration of the facade produces a revulsion against the "bodily fluids and wastes that become condensed with the wounded body in the iconography of misogyny." And women themselves, Mulvey points out, participate in this notion of exterior/interior, of veiled and unveiled. Speaking of how women identify with misogynistic revulsion, not only in adopting the cosmetics of the masquerade but in pathologically at-tempting to expunge the physical marks of the feminine, she says: "The images

Untitled #236, 1987–91. Color photograph, 90 x 60 inches.

of decaying food and vomit raise the specter of the anorexic girl, who tragically acts out the fashion fetish of the female as an eviscerated, cosmetic and artificial construction designed to ward off the 'otherness' hidden in the 'interior.'"[51]

Now, the contrast between interior and exterior, which Mulvey had consumed as the mythic content of Sherman's horizontals, continues to be the thematics she reads into Sherman's work throughout its progression. Moving from the horizontals to the parodically violent fashion images Sherman made in 1983, Mulvey sees these as a protest against the smooth, glossy body of the fashion model, a protest registered by a surface that seems to drop away "to reveal a monstrous otherness behind the cosmetic facade." Or, in the subsequent series inspired by fairy tales she sees the revelation of the very stuff of the unconscious that lines the interior: "While the earlier interiority suggested soft, erotic, reverie, these are materializations of anxiety and dread." Finally in the body's disappearance into the spread of waste and detritus from the late eighties, "the topography of exterior/interior is exhausted," since "these traces represent the end of the road, the secret stuff of bodily fluids that the cosmetic is designed to conceal." With the removal of this final veil and the confrontation of the wound—"the disgust of sexual detritus, decaying food, vomit, slime, menstrual blood, hair"—the fetish fails and with it the very possibility of meaning: "Cindy Sherman traces the abyss or morass that overwhelms the defetishized body, deprived of the fetish's semiotic, reduced to being 'unspeakable' and devoid of significance."[52]

And yet, no sooner is it imagined that the "vomit pictures" have produced the "unspeakable," defetishized body than that body is reprogrammed as the body of the woman: the mother's body from which the child must separate itself in order to achieve autonomy, a separation founded on feelings of disgust against the unclean and the undifferentiated. Using Julia Kristeva's term "abjection" for this preverbal cut into the amorphous and the continuous in order to erect the boundaries between an inside and an outside, a self and an other, Mulvey writes:

> Barbara Creed's argument that abjection is central to the recurring image of the "monstrous feminine" in horror movies is also applica-

ble to the monstrous in Sherman. Although her figures materialize the stuff of irrational terror, they also have pathos and could easily be understood in terms of "the monster as victim." . . . The 1987 series suggests that, although both sexes are subject to abjection, it is women who can explore and analyze the phenomenon with greater equanimity, as it is the female body that has come, not exclusively but predominantly, to represent the shudder aroused by liquidity and decay.[53]

At the very moment, then, when the veil is lifted, when the fetish is stripped away, the mythic content of a packaged signified—"the monstrous feminine"—nonetheless rises into place to occupy the vertical field of the image/form. The truth of the wound is thus revealed. Decoded at last, it reads: the truth of the wound.

But under the hood of the image all the signifiers of the "vomit pictures" are at work to desublimate the visual field. Not only the insistent construction of the /horizontal/ but the sense in which the random glitter of wild light is leering up at the viewer to configure the /unlocatable/ work together to produce a displacement of the body "into the picture" and to install it there as *formless*. This is a field without truth, one that resists being organized in order to produce /the wound/ as its signified. And of course its signifiers are at work, as always, completely in the open, ready for inspection, without a safety net or a veil.

The notion of unveiling what is veiled, of penetrating from exterior to interior is hermeneutical of course, but it is also tied to the psychoanalytic distinction between manifest and latent content. The manifest content of a dream, Freud explained, was its secondary revision, its plausible surface meant to paper over its latent thoughts, the ones that needed to be censored or repressed. The secondary revision is a disguise, a concealment, a veil. In *The Interpretation of Dreams* Freud gives as an example dreams of embarrassment at appearing in public improperly dressed. These he says are veils that cover the dreamer's desire for nakedness, a nakedness that would not produce shame.

Jacques Derrida points to this peculiar slippage between the analytic metaphor of the veil removed to reveal the naked truth and the semantic content in
which the dreamer dreams of a veil that threatens to reveal his nakedness. He
turns to Freud's use of the story of "The Emperor's New Clothes" in this connection. For Freud is illustrating his theory of unveiling the latent contents by
revealing that the hidden theme of the fairy tale is the dream of nakedness, which
is to say, the dream of veiling/unveiling. Objecting that "The Emperor's New
Clothes" is not latently about the dream of nakedness, but manifestly so, and
into the bargain about the act of revelation—staged by the child who calls out,
"But he's naked!"—that itself performs, within the text, the act of veiling/un-
veiling, Derrida writes:

> Freud's text is staged when he explains to us that the text, e.g. that
> of the fairy tale, is an *Einkleidung* [disguise] of the nakedness of the
> dream of nakedness. What Freud states about secondary revision
> (Freud's explaining text) is already staged and represented in advance
> in the text explained (Andersen's fairy tale). This text, *too,* described
> the scene of analysis, the position of the analyst, the forms of his
> language, the metaphorico-conceptual structures of what he seeks
> and what he finds. The locus of one text is in the other.[54]

With this model of the way the form of the inquiry will produce the semantic version, or the thematization, of that very form—veiling/unveiling—as
its *answer,* in an act of finding that always finds itself, Derrida looks at Lacan's use
of a story by Edgar Allan Poe to illustrate his own psychoanalytic theories of
the operations of the signifier. Turning to Lacan's "Seminar on 'The Purloined
Letter,'" Derrida says: "If the critique of a certain sort of semanticism constitutes
an indispensable phase in the elaboration of a theory of the text, the Seminar
exemplifies a clear progress beyond any post-Freudian psychoanalytic critique.
It takes into account the organization, material as well as formal, of the signifier
without throwing itself upon any semantic, not to say thematic, content of the
text."[55]

And yet Derrida will progress from this point toward a demonstration that for Lacan, too, despite his insistence on the materiality of the signifier and on its condition as the mere marker or operator of difference—a differential function that cannot accept the assignment of a fixed meaning—his interpretation of Poe's "Purloined Letter" will constantly move toward an unveiling that will find what it seeks in the place where it expects to find it. It will find, that is, that the letter—the phallic signifier—constructs the fetish: "It is, woman, a place unveiled as that of the lack of the penis, as the truth of the phallus, i.e. of castration. The truth of the purloined letter is the truth itself, its meaning is meaning, its law is law, the contract of truth with itself in the logos."[56]

If Lacan wants to show that in Poe's story the incriminating letter, which the Minister steals from the Queen only, once it is in his possession, to have it ravished from him in turn by Dupin, is the phallus—signifier of the pact that links Queen to King, and signifier as well of castration—so that anyone who possesses it is "feminized," this letter-as-phallus, he insists is a signifier, the circulating operator of meaning, cutting out each character in turn as he or she is submitted to its course. But Derrida argues that far from being the mere differential function of structural linguistics, this letter functions, in fact, as a *transcendental* signifier, which is to say as the term in a series whose ideal and idealizing privilege comes from the fact that it makes the series possible. For Lacan insists not only that the letter-as-phallic-signifier is indivisible and indestructible, but that it has a certain and proper place, the two taken together producing the very truth of the letter: that it will always arrive at its destination, namely, on or at the body of the woman.

The slippage Derrida is interested in is thus a version of the same slippage that had occurred in "The Emperor's New Clothes." For here the notion of pure difference continually returns to the same signified, and the signifying chain with its endless play of signifiers is in fact rooted in place. Thus the analyst is trapped by the very lure of meaningfulness—"it's me!"—that he wishes to analyze. The ideality of the letter-as-phallic-signifier derives from the interpellant system, the one that produces meaning as points of stability between signifiers and signifieds:

———

The idealism which resides in [this system] is not a theoretical position of the analyst, it is a structure-effect of *signification* in general,
whatever transformations or adjustments are practiced on the space
of *semiosis*. It is understandable that Lacan finds this "materiality"
"unique": he retains only its ideality. He considers the letter only at
the point where, determined (whatever he says about it) by its
meaning-content, by the ideality of the message which it "vehicu-
lates," . . . it can circulate, intact, from its place of detachment to the
place of its re-attachment, that is to say, to the same place. In fact,
this letter does not elude only partition, it eludes movement, it does
not change place.[57]

We have seen this before, this result of "the structure-effect of *signification*
in general," which the analyst wants to reveal or unveil but which the analysis
itself repeats by continually setting up the fetish—the Truth of the veil/un-
veiled—in the place of meaning. We have seen this in the analysis of Sherman's
art through all types of mythic consumption, including that of the theory of the
male gaze as production of the eroticized fetish. In all of these there is the continual rush toward the signified, the refusal to follow the signifiers, the steady consumption of the mythic production of meaning.

THE SEX DOLLS

When I did those horizontal pictures of me lying down, I got a lot
of criticism for being "anti-feminist" and "turning the clock back"
by showing these "victims," and these new pictures [the 1985 fairy
tale characters] show me just how wrong I think those people really were.

—*Cindy Sherman*[58]

There may have been many reasons why, in the series she made in 1993,
Sherman turned away from her own body as support for the image and began

to use dolls instead, or more specifically, plastic mannequins acquired from a medical supply house. She had spoken in interviews of trying to imagine breaking away from her own constant presence in front of the camera and possibly using models, although she would always end by saying why it didn't seem feasible.[59] Perhaps she finally found a way to make it feasible; perhaps the decision to stage the display of the genitals and the performance of "sexual acts" was in fact a way of forcing her own body out of the image, giving her an excuse to engage a substitute.

But there are many perhapses. Another has to do with how artists locate themselves in a universe of discourse. Some of the criticism of Sherman that has come from feminists who, unlike Mulvey or Solomon-Godeau, see her not as deconstructing the eroticized fetish but as merely reinstalling it—"Her images are successful partly because they do not threaten phallocracy, they reiterate and confirm it"[60]—has focused on Sherman's silence. By calling every one of her works *Untitled,* they argue, Sherman has taken refuge in a stolid muteness, refusing to speak out on the subject of her art's relation to the issues of domination and submission that are central to feminism. Avoiding interviews as well, it is maintained, Sherman further refuses to take responsibility for the interpretation of her work.

The idea that an artist has a responsibility to come forward with an explicit reading of her or his work seems just as peculiar as the idea that the only way to produce such a reading—should the visual artist wish to do so—would be through words. It is far more usual for artists to construct the interpretive frames within which they are producing and understanding their work by situating themselves in relation to what the critic Mikhail Bakhtin called a discursive horizon. Which is to say that the work an artist makes inevitably enters a field that is structured by other works and their interpretation: the artist can reinforce the dominant interpretation—as when, say, Morris Louis acknowledged the understanding of Pollock's drip paintings as "optical mirages" by paintings his own series of *Veils;* or the artist can resist, and by implication, critique that interpretation—which was the case of Warhol and Morris when they transgressed the optical, modernist reading and, as we saw, produced their own in the form

155

of the horizontalized, urinary trace on the one hand and "anti-form" on the other.

Now the same discursive horizon that is encircling Sherman's work, demanding that it either acknowledge or disconfirm its commitments to feminism, has also held up for criticism, much of it virulent, the work of another artist whose major support is the photographic image. This artist is Hans Bellmer, who spent the years 1934–49, that is, from the rise of the Nazi Party through World War II, in Germany making work to which he gave the series title *La Poupée*. Photographs of dolls that he assembled out of dismountable parts, placing the newly configured body fragments in various situations, mainly domestic, in an early version of installation art, and then disassembling them to start anew, Bellmer's work has been accused of endlessly staging scenes of rape and of violence on the bodies of women.

It thus would seem, within the present discursive horizon, that the act of choosing to make one's art by means of photographing suggestively positioned dolls is, itself, a decision that speaks volumes. Sherman can continue to call these works *Untitled* but they nevertheless produce their own reading through a connection to the *Poupées* of Bellmer.

And this is to say that among other things, they are a statement of what it means to refuse to an artist the work that he or she has done—which is always work on the signifier—and to rush headlong for the signified, the content, the constructed meaning, which one then proceeds to consume as myth. Bellmer's signifiers are—among other things—doll parts. They are not real bodies and they are not even whole bodies. And these signifiers are operated in a way that allows them to slide along the signifying chain, creating the kind of slippage that is meant, precisely, to blur their meaning, rather than to reify it, or better, to create meaning itself as blurred.

Nowhere is this more evident than in an image of four legs attached to a swivel joint that radiate outward along a hay-strewn ground (see fig., p. 27). Unmistakably swastika-like in their configuration, these legs present the viewer with a representation that constructs the Nazi emblem in relation to the scenario of the part-object, in which the body is experienced as being threatened and invaded by dismembering objects. As has been pointed out by Hal Foster in his reading of Bellmer's project, the fascist subject's embrace of the perfect body of the trained soldier and of a hardened neoclassicism has itself been read as a defense against its own sense of menace. That fear of invasion—by a group of others who threaten its borders both geographically (Jews, homosexuals, gypsies, Bolsheviks) and psychically (the unconscious, sexuality, the "feminine")—has been seen in its turn as a projection of a fantasized bodily chaos, the result of a ruined ego construction, a chaos against which the fascist subject armors himself, seeking a defense by means "of the human body."[61]

Seeing Bellmer's project as one that submits itself to sadomasochistic fantasies in order to explore the convulsive tension between binding and shattering and thus to assume a complicity with the fascist subject "only to expose it most effectively," Foster writes: "For in the *poupées* this fear of the destructive and the defusive is made manifest and reflexive, as is the attempt to overcome it in violence against the feminine other—that is a scandal but also a lesson of the dolls."[62]

Bellmer, himself the son of a hated authoritarian father who was indeed a Party member and against whom the *Poupées* can be seen to stage their most flagrant transgression, had written, "If the origin of my work is scandalous, it is because, for me, the world is a scandal." The failure to observe the configuration of the swastika as the ground of reflexiveness from which Bellmer can strike against the father's armor is a failure that allows the semantic naiveté of a description of the work's signified as: a victim of rape.

Just as I would like to think of Sherman in a dialogue with Crimp in the production of *Untitled Film Still #36,* I imagine her reflecting on Foster's argument in the course of producing *Untitled #263.* This is certainly not because I picture her sitting around and reading works of criticism. It is rather because she fully inhabits a discursive space vectored by, among other things, her friends. So that many voices circulate within this space, the supports of many arguments and theories, among them those of Hal Foster.

But the coherence of Sherman's work, something that comes out in retrospect as each succeeding series seems to double back and comment on the earliest

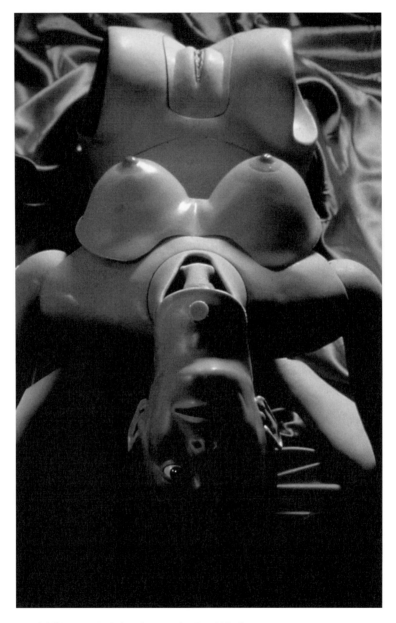

Untitled #261, 1992. Color photograph, 69 x 46 inches.

———

ones, will probably do as much as anything to interpret these images and resolve these "perhapses." Laura Mulvey comments on this effect of Sherman's retrojective meaning: "The visitor [of a Sherman retrospective exhibition] who reaches the final images and then returns, reversing the order, finds that with the hindsight of what was to come, the early images are transformed."[63]

Thus even as this text is going to press, Sherman is undoubtedly making new work. And in that series, or perhaps the next one, we will encounter signifiers that will cut across the discursive horizon and the plane of the image to reinforce and thus to clarify what is even now going on under the hood.

—New York, 1993

Francesca Woodman: Problem Sets

Recounting his role in the development of the teaching system at the Bauhaus, Johannes Itten tells about setting a problem for an advanced group of students by asking them to draw two lemons perched atop a bright green book. Puzzled at the apparent simplemindedness of the exercise, the students whipped off their drawings in a few minutes and sat back to wait. Itten's response was to approach the still-life setup, take one of the lemons, cut it into slices, and pass it out to the students to taste. "Are you sure you've captured the reality of the lemon?" he asked. Smiling in comprehension, they then set back to work.[1]

Two aspects of this story are important in this context. First, there is the existence of the problem set as the vehicle for teaching art throughout practically the whole of this century. And then, there is that matter of "the reality of the lemon," what in Bauhaus language was called Sachlichkeit, or the "world of objectivity." This objectivity was understood to mean the real properties of objects or materials—the hardness, the shininess, the coldness of metal, the roundness and muteness of pebbles, the rhythm-within-variation of wood grain—and the laws of color and of form.

That these properties are both formal and objective, that they are what an artist searches for beneath the happenstance of appearance, that there are equally objective rules of compositional harmonics or of contrast, that there is in short a formal language that can be both learned and spoken, this is the pedagogical legacy of modernism. It is a kind of training that staves off subjectivity as long as possible, that dreads a too-early fall into the purely personal.

Among the five hundred or so photographs that comprise the oeuvre of Francesca Woodman are many that remain in their original presentation format for reviews in her classes at RISD. Still mounted in their cardboard mats, they often bear the titles of those problem sets that are intended to introduce the rules of the most basic stock-in-trade of the photographer. We find "Depth of Field" penciled below the bottom left corner of some of them; "Point of View," or "Three Kinds of Melons in Four Kinds of Light," or "Charlie the Model," or "On Being an Angel" announce what sounds like the problem sets of other assignments. In certain cases the original problem and its relation to the skills a photographer must develop are obvious; in other cases we must infer, although without too much difficulty, what the point of the exercise might have been.[2] The tenfold series called "Charlie the Model" is structured as if it were imagined as the response to a portrait assignment: something like "Photograph someone you know in a way that will bring out his or her customary actions and gestures." The much smaller group, titled "On Being an Angel," could have been a way of answering the problem "Is it possible to photograph something that doesn't exist?" Or the series called "Space²," which was undoubtedly made in fulfillment of a studio assignment, might have been devised as a reply to something like "Define a particular space by emphasizing its character, its geometries, for example."

Woodman's response to this last problem is characteristic of the way she worked, not only as a student, but later as a photographer after she left RISD. She internalized the problem, subjectivized it, rendered it as personal as possible.

Her "Space Squared" became a glass and wood display case found in the storerooms of the museum, with a naked body crouched inside it pressing against one of its panes, in a gesture of mute imprisonment. Or again, that same case, now more centered within the frame of the image, captures the crouching body blurred in a haze of light, another body draped across the top of the case as a kind of pedimental figure emphasizing the architecture of this peculiar cage of

From *Space²*, 1975–76. Silver print. Providence.

From *Space²*, 1975–76. Silver print. Providence.

glass. Or, in a third way of imagining the subject: a display case filled with stuffed animals divides the frame of the photograph into the geometrical packages of its sections and their shelves. The upper-left quadrant shows us gulls, the right one a fox, the lower left a raccoon, the lower-right a "disturbance," as the rectilinear pane of the case's door rotates slightly out of alignment with the face of the image, mirroring unexplainable reaches of the room in front of it, pushed open by the pressure of the head of a girl—Woodman herself—spilling out of the vitrine, her hair tumbling onto the floor of the room.

One of the sensations one has in looking at these examples is amazement at the dispatch with which the formal, "objective," part of the problem is dispensed with—a dispatch that is also a kind of giddy brilliance. The geometry of the three-dimensional world must be made to acknowledge the two-dimensional parameters of the print, must be reconciled to the flatness of the photographer's optical ground. The pressure of those bodies, turning all architectural edges into surrogate frames that contain, flatten, delimit; that use of glass to refer to the supposed "transparency" to reality of the photographic medium even while de-vising means to render it opaque; that constant reference to the inner laws of the photograph as it stills motion and holds its contents in eternal display: all these things are acknowledgments of the formal constraints that "square" a space, aligning it ever more tightly with the conditions of the Rolex's field—itself a square.

But those are "merely" the objective dimensions of the problem as Wood-man chose here to read it. The real conceptual pressure of the problem starts somewhere else . . . with the meaning of a cage for the body it holds. That is space really squared, no? What does it feel to be on display? What does "forever" feel like? What would it be like to be, eternally, the center of someone's gaze?

One can almost hear the inner laughter that must have greeted the unspo-ken decorum of the pedagogical task. Objectivity is fine; but without the subjec-tive, the personal, there simply is no problem.

"Charlie the Model" brings home the way the objective language is both never out of sight and never quite the point. The first print in the series bears the inscription "Charlie has been a model at RISD for 19 years. I guess he knows a lot about being flattened to fit paper." The image so captioned shows the corner of a classroom where a man in pants and a T-shirt, holding a pane of glass in front of him, bends to regard his own image framed in a large wall-mirror. In the second image Charlie has shed his clothes and, framed between the mirror of one of the room's walls and a window defining the plane of the other, he holds a large sketch page before him on which we see the efforts of one of the painting students to render Charlie's familiar girth, his genial nudity. Charlie himself lifts a leg in mock imitation of the pose. Holding a long sheet of paper in front of him in the third image, he whips it to one side in the fourth, where it appears as a phantom haze not quite registered by the just-too-slow exposure, a blur of light misaligned with the frame of the window. The caption says, "There is the paper and then there is the person."

But since "the person" always seemed, within the work of art, to entail risk, that is not a danger to which Woodman seemed to be able to expose another. And so, seven images into the set we see Woodman herself, first clothed, instructing Charlie on the pose, surrounded by the props of the series: the pane of glass, the hand-held mirror, the round fishbowl; then, in the succeeding pair, she too is naked, her own nudity something blurred and nervous, dancing around Charlie's stolid ability to hold the pose, to give himself to the "paper."

For Woodman, this giving oneself to the paper was both the *meaning* of the pose *and* the conditions of the "objective language" of the medium—conditions that are serious, even grim, if really considered, if taken quite literally. Everything that one photographs is in fact "flattened to fit" paper, and thus under, within, permeating, every paper support, there is a body. And this body may be in extremus, may be in pain. The last entry in the "Charlie the Model" series refers to death. We see Charlie spread-eagled in the darkened corner, the pane of glass pressing against his chest. It is not visually a very pleasant image; there is too much shadow for it to read. But the caption goes, "Sometimes things seem very dark. Charlie had a heart attack. I hope things get better for him."

The pair of prints "Horizontale" and "Verticale"—made at RISD—demonstrate once again the subjectification of the objective language, the immediate

Charlie the Model #4, 1976–77. Silver print. Providence.

Charlie the Model #5, 1976–77. Silver print. Providence.

Charlie the Model #8, 1976–77. Silver print. Providence.

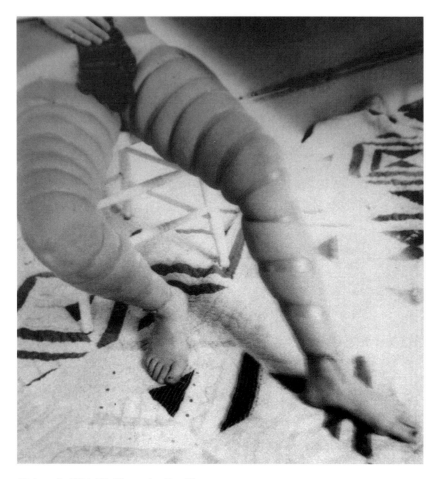

Horizontale, 1976–77. Silver print. Providence.

Verticale, 1976–77. Silver print. Providence.

instinct to register the formal within the "support" of the body. In the problem-set mentality you are asked to create a formal pair, like depth/surface, figure/frame/, horizontal/vertical. What would you think of? As a photographer, what would you start to do? Woodman thought about the body's assumption of those dimensions—not so much as a field of action: stretching, leaping, floating, lying down—but as a field of inscription. In one print we see a kneeling figure whose lower torso nearly fills the frame. She is clothed in black, striped tights, their striations running vertically along the length of the legs and thighs toward her waist. Hanging by her side, one arm holds the verticality of the pose, the other shakes itself into a blur of horizontal motion.

In the mate to this image, the figure is seated on a low stool, and once more we only see her from about waist down. But now her legs, stretched before her, are tightly wrapped in bands of plastic that circle her flesh every several inches, alternating ligatures and indecent bulges. Yet because this apparition extends from the upper-left corner of the frame to its lower-right, the direction of these bindings is complicated by a diagonal condition, just as the moving hand in the first print had counteracted the too pat verticality of the stripes.

Always to insert her own body onto the field of the problem, to use it, understand it, as the ground of whatever sense the image might make, is the pattern that emerges throughout the problem sets that Woodman undertook. "House" is another series, whether assignment or not we will not know. Perhaps at some point the students were asked to picture something familiar, their own rooms, for example. The response of "House" is to take a dilapidated space, a house within which the paint is flaking, the wallpaper peeling off in long paste-stiffened strips, the floorboards warped and the plaster falling. But these things are not really the objects of vision. They are not what is examined. They are what is used as surrogate surfaces, the elements that flatten someone "to fit paper." For everywhere in the field we make out the figure of Woodman: crouched behind the framelike facade of a mantel, hidden by a great curl of wallpaper, vanishing into the flattening haze of a window embrasure. Just out of sight, she is the field of experience, tiny, fragile, slid just beneath the skin.

At some later time one of the members of "House" was recruited as a member of a different series, a narrative about no longer playing the piano. On the reverse side of one of the prints of this new grouping, Woodman jotted a note as much to her classmates as to herself. "The way things went," she wrote. "I kept trying to change my direction and photograph other things. Man I am as tired as the rest of you of looking at me. . . ."

But this sentiment comes across as mere self-consciousness, as though she suddenly thought about what it must look like to others to translate every problem onto the field of her own person. In fact there is nothing narcissistic about this transferring of the formal to the plane of the personal, this inscribing of the objective language onto the surface of her own back. The image that left "House" to join the piano narrative is the one that shows Woodman crouching, face to the wall, behind a broad swatch of peeled-away wallpaper, most of her body invisible except for a tiny part of her hip and her arms and hands pressed before her onto the plane of the wall. The inscription under this print, the fourth in the series, follows the captions that had read: "I stopped playing the piano . . . And I had forgotten how to read music, . . . I could no longer play/I could not play by instinct." This image now bears the words "Then at one point I did not need to translate the notes; they went directly to my hands." Nothing could be more precise about a sense of self as a medium, a conduit, a plane of passage.

That Woodman's instincts within this activity were both incredibly direct and incredibly sure are evidenced throughout her work. Asked no doubt to photograph a non-existent being, she thought, perhaps, of Courbet's realist remark, "I'll paint an angel when I see one!" And contorting herself into a position where she rises out of the bottom frame of the field, her body leads with her uptilted breasts opening out into the image of so many improbable wings, her umbrella in the back of the empty room appearing to float in the space above her. As she makes "On Being an Angel," she might have said, "I'll see an angel when I'll be one."

The problem set is deeply ingrained into the thinking of artists throughout the twentieth century. Françoise Gilot, for example, tells of being sent problems

On Being an Angel, Spring 1977. Silver print. Providence.

From *Angel Series,* September 1977. Silver print. Rome.

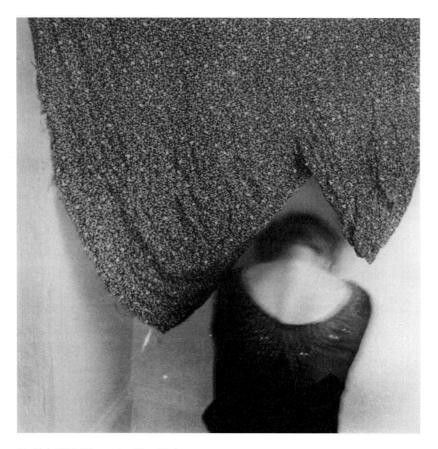

Untitled, 1980. Silver print. New York.

by Picasso. "Sometimes he would have me do things for composition," she writes.

> He would give me a piece of blue paper—perhaps a cigarette wrapper—and a match, tear off a piece of cardboard and say, "Make me a composition with those. Organize them for me into this," and he would draw a form on a piece of paper to indicate the size and shape.[3]

It is hard to imagine the Picasso of the 1940s involved in problem sets, so abandoned had he become to the turbulent inner theater of his obsessional preoccupations—psychological, erotic, fantastic. But of course none of this ever occluded the "objective language" that would speak these obsessions.

The problem set seems to have been something Woodman deeply respected even while she surpassed its limited terms again, and again. In Rome, she took up anew the series "On Being an Angel," pushing it toward a different experience of the real as embodied. The problem set had become a medium in which to think, in which to work.

—New York, 1986

Sherrie Levine: Bachelors

The unpleasant thing, and one that nags at my modesty, is that at root *every name in history is I.*

—Deleuze and Guattari, quoting Nietzsche

"I always wanted," she said, "to find a way to make sculpture. . . . What I wanted was to be able to make a sculpture." And what had he said, a quarter of a century ago now? "I wanted to make a railroad car," he wrote from Voltri, in 1962. "Given enough time I could have made a train." David Smith, however, was already a sculptor; the "way" he wanted to find was not on the order of how to make the object, but how to make its phallic import absolutely unmistakable, even to himself.

So these two desires—to make a sculpture, to make a train—are different desires, we might say; they are the effects of different orders of fantasy.

But why, you could ask, would Sherrie Levine need to "find a way" to make a sculpture? Isn't the strategy of the ready-made (her adoptive strategy, after all) itself, in fact, already a way of making sculpture? The series of things it produces—the snow shovel, the bottle rack, the urinal, the comb—are already part of the order of the freestanding object; even his calendar (*Pharmacy*) and the advertisement he "corrected" (*Apollinaire Enameled*) enter the world of the ready-made as *objects* rather than images. And so her grids, painted on lead, are likewise displaced from the domain of the image. Through the strategy of the ready-made they are reinvented as chessboards, as checkerboards, as objects. If she called her early, pirated photographs "collages," it is because the image, scissored out of the pages of an art book, acquires along with its status as a ready-made, the reified condition of the object.

But the difference between the (ready-made) object and the sculpture may be this: that the sculpture makes it absolutely unmistakable, even to us, that the world of things to which it belongs is that of the "part-object." It has not come from off the shelf, of supermarket, or department store, or bookshop. There is no question but that it has migrated off the body: so many detachable organs, so many areas of intensity, the effects of so many proper names. The series: Rodin, Maillol, Duchamp, Brancusi, and closer to us, Morris, Andre, Hesse. So many names to which to attach the effect of a desire for the part-object: breast, penis, eye, hand, anus. The Rodin effect we could call it, the Brancusi effect, the Duchamp effect.

It was in 1952 that Michel Carrouges isolated the Duchamp effect. He called it "the bachelor machine," and he linked it to another series of names: Franz Kafka's mechanism for torture through tattooing, in *The Penal Colony;* Villier de l'Isle Adam's irresistible automaton, in *The Eve of the Future;* Raymond Roussel's machines for textual production, in *Impressions of Africa*.[1] The model of the machine was clearest, most complete, however, in *The Bride Stripped Bare by Her Bachelors, Even.* Everything was there: the plan for perpetual motion that the "Litanies" chanted as "vicious circle"; the complexity of the interconnections (glider, malic molds, sieves, chocolate grinder, scissors . . .); the sterility of the cycle, its autoeroticism, its narcissism; the utter self-enclosure of the system, in which desire is at one and the same time producer, consumer, and re-producer (recorder or copier), which is to say, the bachelor apparatus, the oculist witnesses, the top inscription of the bride.

In 1972 the bachelor machine was there, waiting, for Gilles Deleuze and Félix Guattari to hook it up to the body without organs, to plug it into the logic of the desiring machines, to reinvent the Duchamp effect within the world of schizo-capitalism.[2] The total interconnectedness of the machines and the absolute deterritorialization of the world onto which they cling: an undifferentiated *socius,* the body without organs, the subject without a center, the world without Oedipus.

The bachelor machine of *Anti-Oedipus* constructs the relationship between the desiring machines and the body without organs, between the bachelor's world of production and the bride's domain of inscription. The desiring machines produce by intercepting the continuous flows of milk, urine, semen, shit; they interrupt one flow in order to produce another, which the next machine will interrupt to produce a flow for the next, and so on. Each machine is a part-object: the breast-machine, the mouth-machine, the stomach-machine, the intestine-machine, the anus-machine. As opposed to this the body without organs produces nothing; it re-produces. It is the domain of simulation, of series crossing one another, of the possible occupation of every place in the series by a subject forever decentered. "I am Prado, I am also Prado's father. I venture to say that I am also Lesseps. . . . I wanted to give my Parisians, whom I love, a new idea—that of a decent criminal. I am also Chambige—also a decent criminal. . . . The unpleasant thing, and one that nags at my modesty, is that at root *every name in history is I.*"[3] The body without organs is the place of inscription; it is textual, semiological. But its logic is not that of the signifier, that of representation. Rather it is the logic of flows of information in which the content of the first flow (its product) is the expressive medium of the second (its producer). Deleuze and Gauttari quote McLuhan here: "The electric light is pure information. It is a medium without a message, as it were, unless it is used to spell out some verbal ad or name. This fact, characteristic of all media, means that the content of any medium is always another medium. The content of writing is speech, just as the written word is the content of print, and print is the content of the telegraph."[4] The same logic is at work, then, within the world of production—the desiring machines—and that of consumption and re-production— the body without organs. That is the achievement of the bachelor machine; it holds up the mirror in which the blossoming of the bride reflects onto the

---

cemetery of the uniforms and liveries, in which the inscription is the same as the production, a place where the erotic energy of the "shots" is locked forever in a "mirrorical return." The bachelor machine produces this folding of the one over the other as a moment of pure intensity.

In 1989 the bachelor machine was there, waiting, to provide Sherrie Levine with "a way" to make sculpture. The Duchamp effect she needed was not that of the ready-made, which describes the relations among commodities, and between commodities and their consumers, but that of the bachelor-machine, which invokes the connections between part-objects. And the malic molds, otherwise called the cemetery of uniforms and liveries, would provide these part-objects "ready-made." The "way to make a sculpture" would be to exhume them, to liberate them from the plane of *The Large Glass,* to cast them in three dimensions. By freeing them from their connection in the series: sieves-malic molds-capillary tubes-glider-chocolate grinder. . . , they would be liberated ever more securely into the other series: Rodin-Maillol-Brancusi-Duchamp-Hesse. . . , the series that includes David Smith most clearly when he dreams of wanting to make a train.

And nothing needs to be added to these bachelors. They are just as Duchamp left them, ready-made. Not as he made them, for on the field of *The Bride Stripped Bare by Her Bachelors, Even* they are in the two dimensions of sheets of lead; but as he projected them, within the notes he so patiently stored in *The Green Box.* For he envisioned them as molds after all, and therefore to be cast. Each cast producing a bachelor, or as he would also put it, a malic form. And the contents of the molds he described as well, when he imagined the illuminating gas inside the molds as solidifying into frosty spangles—"a thousand spangles of frosty gas." To cast the bachelors in glass, and then to frost the glass, is therefore to add nothing, to create nothing. It is to accept Duchamp's bachelors, his malic forms, ready-made. It is to do nothing more than to occupy that historical position that can be called the Duchamp effect.

The only thing here that is added to the Duchamp effect is what is subtracted, namely, the effect of cutting away the bachelors from the rest of the apparatus, from the glider, the sieves, the grinder, the scissors, the splashes. . . , and finally of separating each bachelor from his fellows. The isolation is what is added. It is, we could say, an added subtraction. So that the question is how to characterize this excision that the artist's own desiring machine produces within the connected flow of Duchamp's apparatus, of Duchamp's glass?

One answer is that the added subtraction equals "lack." Desire, according to this, desires what is absent. It wants to have the missing thing. And that thing that is missing will, by giving lack its name, also give desire its meaning. In this reading the sculpture occupies the level of a fantasy. It stays within the world of representation as the model of something desired. Its lack is castrative; its meaning is redemptive, meaning redeemed. It is sculpture as the desire for meaning.

But another answer is that the added subtraction allows the bachelor, now cast in glass, actually to be produced, and thus to be added to the domain of reality. The bachelor does not mark the place of lack but rather the site of production. And within this production it forms a series, for it is produced in multiple. It creates a flow of little glass replicas, the continuum of the series that the machine now slices apart, making one little thing after the other. And, actualized within this production, it enters the whole array of other, similar, series:

1. The art-historical series: lying recumbent, like the gleaming bronze eggs of Brancusi, it attaches itself to them, as so many infantile moments of contentment, so many breasts, mouths, bellies.

2. The aesthetic series: sheltering within its little, glass vitrine, it is like the fragments of antiquity displayed in a museum—so many torsos, legs, arms, shoulders. Which means its glass case becomes a museum-machine, interrupting the flow of the antique *Kunstindustrie*—the fifth-, fourth-, third-century circulation of multiples within the classical decorative-arts production—isolating and creating the neoclassical fragment, the aestheticized form of modernist sculpture as a desire for the part-object.

3. The formal series: a series within a series, it is the glass container inside the glass container of its case, reproducing itself in ever smaller miniaturizations, glass as the form of transparency, as form *en abîme*.

———

Untitled (The Bachelors: "Gendarme"), 1989. Glass, 10 x 4 x 3 3/4 inches.

Untitled (The Bachelors: "Larbin"), 1989. Glass, 12 x 5 x 5 inches.

Untitled (The Bachelors: "Croque-mort"), 1989. Glass, 11 1/4 x 5 1/4 x 3 inches.

Untitled (The Bachelors: "Cuirassier"), 1989. Glass, 12 1/2 x 5 1/2 x 3 1/4 inches.

Untitled (The Bachelors: "Gardien de la paix"), 1989. Glass, 10 1/2 x 11 x 4 1/2 inches.

Untitled (The Bachelors: "Livreur de grand magasin"), 1989. Glass, 10 x 2 1/2 x 2 1/2 inches.

4. The commodity series: "The question of shop windows," Duchamp had written, "/ . . . The exigency of the shop window/ The shop window proof of the existence of the outside world." Desiring production and economic production are not metaphors for one another, *Anti-Oedipus* insists; their relation is not that of representation. Their connection is real.

It is the very isolation of each of Levine's *Bachelors* that allows us to plot the array of its possible connections, to see it not only as the little phallic part-object, the desiring machine, but also as the slippery, undifferentiated surface of the closed form, *Anti-Oedipus*'s body without organs, the locus of desire as an endless play of substitutions. And it is onto this deterritorialized body that the Levine effect can be plotted, produced.

The little Joey of Bruno Bettelheim's *Empty Fortress* announces his own occupation within the labyrinth of the bachelor machine. "Connecticut, Connect-I-cut," he cries. All of his life functions, Joey claims, will only work if he is plugged into machines that will, with their motors whirring and their lights blinking, allow him to breathe, to eat, to defecate. "Connect-I-cut" is Joey's rare instance of the first person, of "I." Mostly he is a third person, a function of the machine. He is an effect of the machines, rather than a subject. The Joey effect.

To release desire into a world without a subject, a world in which proper names form a series among themselves, a world in which the name claims nothing, "means" nothing, even though it continues to produce: this is a description of the Levine effect.

—Belle-Ile-en Mer, 1989

Louise Lawler: Souvenir Memories

I

We begin with the assumption of spectacle. It is there in the idea of an exhibition that will include slide projections to be seen at night through the storefront window of a gallery, the miragelike image hovering in the darkened space like an exhibitionistic ghost. It is there in the display of the paperweights, in their combined references to the jewelry store and the peep show. For if the jewelry store is signaled by the rows of chest-high pedestals with their Plexiglas tops, within which the little crystal half-globes are on show as so many identically precious objects, the peep show is triggered by the action of the objects' semispherical "lenses" which narrow down the viewer's gaze to an almost impossibly small point of entry into the work's visual field he or she must hunch over to see— Duchamp's *Etant donnés* rewritten as tiny, kitsch souvenirs.

Making works of art whose supports are consistently drawn from the lowest rungs of commodity culture, from matchbooks, from dime-store glassware, but also from the visual vocabularies of journalistic and commercial photography, Louise Lawler's relation to these supports is not ironic but meditative, almost loving. Onto the shiny red covers of a set of matchbooks she letters the subheadings from Roland Barthes's *A Lover's Discourse*—"angoisse," "askesis," "corps"—

External Simulation View at Night, 1994. Metro Pictures Gallery, New York.

External Simulation, installation view, 1994.

hand-setting each letter meticulously in preparation for the hot-stamping of the type in foil. She photographs a Pollock hanging over a dining room sideboard; the picture is pure *House & Garden* or *Vogue Interiors,* half soup-tureen, half violently dripped canvas; but she has so effaced herself before the spectacle language that it is hard to find the anger or the contempt or any of the other avant-garde modes of outrage in the image. She photographs a wall from the showroom at Sotheby's installed for a contemporary art auction; the picture is strangely cropped so that while we notice the glassy varnish on the surface of a Warhol whose contents we can therefore barely discern, our noses are also pressed against the stains and dirt of the carpet-lined walls and the crooked, tattered card that hawks this painting as so much merchandise. Siding momentarily with photo-journalism, Lawler's image then relapses, however, into the strangely stunned but tender neutrality that one would have to identify as her "style."

II

That style takes the condition of spectacle as a fact of life. Writing in the 1930s, Walter Benjamin had imagined the revolutionary effect—whether for good or evil—of photographic reproduction on the work of art, the "destruction of its aura," both in terms of its condition as unique, and its embeddedness in a tradition of rich associations, by delivering the aesthetic image to the system of its own replication and dissemination: what would later come to be called "sign exchange." But however vivid his imagination, Benjamin could not know what it would be like for these effects to have become the totality of one's experience. He could not know the degree to which the oppositions that run through his own work, structuring its logic—oppositions such as those between the storyteller and the journalist, or the collector and the consumer—would collapse under the simulacral force of spectacle.

What Lawler takes for granted is the result of this force and its absolute pervasiveness. It is no longer the case that painting has a resistant opacity—due to its material presence, its objectifiable surface—while photography is nothing but the pure transparency of a slippery illusionism through which we are sucked into the half-truths of the world of media. Under the pressures of spectacle, the logic of this opposition has become warped into something that looks more like a pretzel or a Möbius strip than it does a straightforward binary. For, within the conditions of a culture of the spectacle, the values of opacity and transparency have, it would seem, changed places. As Andy Warhol had already made perfectly clear, media has constructed its own supposedly transparent world as a space entirely peopled by commodities (the Marilyns, the Jackies, the Elvises), so that the signs that circulate within it are as opaque and depthless as one could want. And on the other hand, the conditions of reproduction, as they seep across the boundary into high art, a boundary they have rendered altogether porous, have turned every gesture and every seemingly resistant surface of painting into the glitteringly transparent sign of its own subordination to a spectacle world in which it no longer operates in relation to values like spontaneity or authenticity, but functions as a pure token of sign exchange.

And there is another transformation that has become a corollary of this: if the opacity of the modernist pictorial surface was an index of the materiality of the picture plane, it acted to force that plane onto a level continuous with other physical bodies thereby declaring the work of art a function of public space. The displacement of that index into the world of reproductions—where the gesture is always already an image of itself—is a function of the solipsism of media, of a condition of spectacle that means that its public is impossibly dispersed and privatized, each viewer isolated in front of a television set, each positioned at the aperture of the peep show. This too is the work of what we could call the photographic as it operates on all the arts.

To assume this condition of spectacle as the very texture of one's own world, the fabric of one's very sensibility, is to observe that world through the eyes of spectacle. It is to see everything mutate into at least two versions of itself: the "original" object and the sign for that object, although within the logic of spectacle's mirror reflections it is never clear which is which. The gleams and reflections that interest Lawler, as she photographs works of modernist art within their present condition of commodification—a Frank Stella "protractor" painting, for example, photographed as nothing but its own rainbowlike reflection in the polished floor of its display space—are avatars of this pervasive condition of the sign.

But it is not only recent art that is so infected. As Lawler photographs the salon of a Swiss collector, its decorous little tables and chairs seem to have migrated from the world of rarefied antiques and to have entered the space of the reproduction, the elegant room now resembling nothing so much as an upper-class hotel lobby. But even more disconcertingly, the two paintings by Ferdinand Hodler that dominate the salon undergo the same internal mutation. For Hodler has pictured three pairs of lovers, two in one painting, one in the other, their bodies locked together in turn-of-the-century symbolist erotic intensity. Each of the pairings is slightly different, an index of the measure to which lovers are unique in each other's eyes, revered with feelings that are never-to-be-duplicated, or repeated. Looking at this display through Lawler's gaze—so attentive and yet so dispassionate—what we see is not the uniqueness of these pairs but their repetition, each becoming the redoubled sign of the other, as though despite whatever he had intended, Holder had flattened and debased and emptied out his own world.

III

It is the photograph of the "Hodler salon" that stands sentinel over Lawler's subsequent displays of the paperweights (one of which contains the "Hodler salon" in miniature) as a series. Using as their vehicle, the kitsch-level, mass-cultural object, these works enact their relation to photography not only in their obvious condition as multiples, but more interestingly in the way each crystal half-sphere presents itself as a lens, one through which one peers as though through a camera's viewfinder. And by means of that line of sight, that unifocal vector, one is summoned to perform on *this* side of the lens the very closing out of public space that has emerged as the result of the mediated world of photography. Substituting for the shared space within which culture formerly operated, a position that can only be occupied by one viewer at a time, the lens enforces a situation in which the only public thing that can occur in the space in which

Untitled (Salon Hodler), 1992. Cibachrome, crystal, and felt, 2 x 3 1/2 inches.

Write a story, do, about a young man, the son of a serf, a former grocery boy, a choirsinger, a high school pupil and university student, brought up to respect rank, to kiss the hands of priests, to truckle to the ideas of others—a young man who expressed thanks for every piece of bread, who was whipped many times, who went without galoshes to do his tutoring, who used his fists, tortured animals, was fond of dining with rich relatives, was a hypocrite in his dealing with God and men, needlessly, solely out of a realization of his own insignificance—write how this young man squeezes the slave out of himself, drop by drop, and how, on awaking one fine morning, he feels that the blood coursing through his veins is no longer that of a slave but that of a real human being.

—Anton Chekhov in a letter to a young writer

these works are displayed is a form of voyeurism in which one either watches someone else looking or takes one's own visual pleasure with the concomitant sensation of being watched.

And on the *other* side of the lens, the one that gathers a world of objects into its view, what we encounter is a kind of brilliant summary of the lessons Walter Benjamin read to us in his various essays on photography—lessons about photography's bringing far away things close to us, miniaturizing them for us so as to give us a sense of possessing them. Lessons as well about how photography would utterly transform art, forcing it to renounce its earlier cult-value and even its subsequent exhibition-value for a new, modern, post-photographical value, which he linked to documentary. Benjamin had high hopes, of course, for the revolutionary potential of this documentary, hopes that Lawler does not allow herself, here, to share. But the documentation she nonetheless brings us is about the fate of art in the private spaces of its commodification as it is also about the fate of the museum. For the little half-orb of the paperweight produces its own counterdiscourse about the museum's stated ambitions to assemble disparate objects into a single space and to bestow on them the intellectual, aesthetic, and categorical coherence of a collection, conserving these objects for posterity, one symbol for which is the obsessive placing of them under glass.

Yet even while it announces the shriveling and diminution of these aspirations within the trivialization of the spectacle world, this symbol also reminds us of the utopian aspects of the museum's early project insofar as the museum presented an original that in its material presence seemed to oppose itself, all the way down the line, to the simulacral drive of photography. And, indeed, what one could call the utopian dimension of Lawler's paperweight objects is that they are never completely or satisfactorily open to their own photographic reproduction: the lens producing, here, its own form of opacity and thus of resistance. Thus it is somewhere in the thickness of the works' orbs of crystal—part photographic lens, part vitrine, part protective glazing—that these two fates—art's and photography's—have met and become intertwined. And strangely, photography seems now to have taken up the cause of art's presumed uniqueness, its supposed resistance to commodification both at the level of the object and at the level

Untitled (Collection of 60 Drawings), 1992/93. Cibachrome, crystal, and felt, 2 x 3 1/2 inches.

Untitled, 1989. Cibachrone, crystal, and felt, 2 x 3 1/2 inches.

of its conditions of viewing. Which is to say that this paradoxical form of the photograph—itself never completely reproducible—seems to have taken up the cause of uniqueness and at the same time to be showing it to us from an extraordinary distance, bodying forth what might be seen as the sensuous equivalent of what we could call the past.

IV

When Walter Benjamin writes about the collector, setting this figure against the consumer—as an endangered species to be contrasted with a wildly multiplying weed—this opposition turns around a shared spatial metaphor, that of the case or vitrine or protective covering itself set within a private interior. For commodity culture has provided the consumer with objects that come in ever proliferating casings—the cozies, the bell jars, the upholstery guards—that "house" the various bibelots and specialty items so necessary to the bourgeois home. Spinning around itself its own version of that housing in miniature, the commodity thereby takes on a "human" character, becoming a little microcosm of that subjectivity-set-within-an-interior which is itself proposed as the model of the bourgeois subject's autonomy, its independence from the instrumentalized world of public space. Yet the same delusive notion of subjectivity that operates for the commodity operates for its owner, since as Benjamin argues, the bourgeois apartment is not in fact the image of the renter's freedom but instead of his powerlessness, of the fact that he no longer owns the means of production.

The sense in which the collector opposes this structure is that, for Benjamin, his acquisition of objects is precisely a means of giving them their liberty, of removing them both from the condition of use and the structure of exchange by imbedding them into a matrix of memory. "One has only to watch a collector handle the objects in his glass case," Benjamin writes. "As he holds them in his hands, he seems to be seeing through them into their distant past as though inspired. So much for the magical side of the collector—his old-age image, I might call it"; or again, "to a book collector the true freedom of all books is somewhere on his shelves" ("Unpacking My Library").

But even as the true collector performs this ritual of liberating the objects in his collection, the consumer debases that gesture by giving it its commodity form, since the consumer's collecting consists in nothing more than "packaged" memories in the form of souvenirs. Souvenirs that come in many guises, one persistent one being the image/object crystallized within the glass dome of the paperweight.

That these objects of Lawler's should be complicitous with the commodified form of memory is continuous with the orbit of spectacle culture within which she locates her works. But it is here that the peculiar affect of her style— its quiet lack of outrage, its absence of the judgmental—produces that same utopian moment, however brief, that registers in the crystalline lens's polyvalence as well. For the experience of stunned immobility she produces, while it might be shared by the subject of spectacle, is also characteristic of a quite different subject, one whom Walter Benjamin had in mind when he celebrated the collector as a vanishing breed. Because in speaking about the glass cases in which his rarefied objects are stored, it is not the art *amateur* that Benjamin is picturing so much as it is a figure who ultimately joins hands with a far older form of collector, reaching back to the beginnings of collecting in the sixteenth century's addiction to the Wunderkammer. This is the ultimate model for Benjamin: those cabinets in which were stored strange assortments of natural and other "wonders," which Francis Bacon described as "whatsoever the hand of man by exquisite art or engine has made rare in stuff, form or motion; whatsoever singularity, chance and the shuffle of things hath produced; whatsoever Nature has wrought in things that want life and may be kept." Typical of such a collection would the following items from Sir Walter Cope's cabinet: a Madonna made of feathers, a chain made of monkey teeth, stone shears, the horn and tail of a rhinoceros, the horn of a bull seal, a round horn that had grown on an Englishwoman's forehead, a phosphorescent bird, etc.

This list makes it clear that the prize of these objects has nothing to do with the intrinsic preciousness of their supports nor with any form of value deriving from a system that could be thought to be aesthetic. Rather, as the name implies, it is the sensation of wonder elicited by these objects that is what unites them in their otherwise unfathomable heterogeneity, a sensation that Stephen Greenblatt in *Marvelous Possessions: The Wonder of the New World* connects to the sudden influx of strange objects brought back to Europe from the Americas. "Columbus's voyage initiated a century of intense wonder," he writes, adding: "European culture experienced something like the 'startle reflex' one can observe in infants: eyes widened, arms outstretched, breathing stilled, the whole body momentarily convulsed." Implicit in this assimilation of the startle reflex to wonder is the sense that these marvels themselves belonged by definition to no "tradition," and thus imposed themselves on the consciousness of Europe as objects deprived of aura.

The easiest reaction one can have to the disparate assortments Lawler documents as she tracks works of art back to their present spaces of "private" consumption, where they join the sleek jumble of domestic or commercial furnishings as so much expensive décor, is that of contempt for the collectors who now subject this art to a set of debased functions. But another reaction, Lawler also teaches us, is possible as well. It is far less judgmental and in so being opens the image up to that stunned immobility that can be associated with wonder.

Consider the image, entirely typical of Lawler's work, that puts the collector's power of "composing" on display as it frames a section of a room in such a way as to underscore the arrangement of rectangles formed by paintings (Joseph Beuys, a Japanese screen) and furniture (chair back, side table) hung on or set against the background of a geometrically wood-paneled wall, the objects themselves truncated, Manet-style, by the framing edge of the photograph. However, going beyond the mere sense that such a composition is a patchwork constituted by disparate objects (paintings and furniture) is the presence, on the side table, of a large petrified fungus polished and inlaid with bronze ornaments and a lamp fabricated from an African bronze utensil, its handle wreathed in cowry shells. It is this identification that ranges itself on the side of wonder, thereby opening the collection backward toward the fragility and precariousness of a cultural past,

It Could Be Elvis, 1994/96. Black and white photograph with text on mat, 28 x 30 inches.

one that had from its very inception threaded the pillage of the new world together with the transfixed opening up to the fresh domains of human consciousness which that bounty also induced.

If Lawler's camera documents the contemporary collector's powers to compose, a power that implies everywhere a force of subjugation, it also—in the very stillness and distance of its gaze—puts wonder in place. No matter how temporarily and with what ambivalence.

—New York, 1996

NOTES

CHAPTER 1: CLAUDE CAHUN AND DORA MAAR: BY WAY OF INTRODUCTION

1. I developed this initially in a discussion of surrealist objects and their relation to David Smith's concept of totemism, in *Terminal Iron Works: The Sculpture of David Smith* (Cambridge: MIT Press, 1971), 125ff.

2. Xavière Gauthier, *Surréalisme et sexualité* (Paris: Gallimard, 1971).

3. See, for example, Susan Rubin Suleiman, "Transgression and the Avant-Garde: Bataille's *Histoire de l'oeil, Subversive Intent* (Cambridge: Harvard University Press, 1990); Mary Anne Caws, Rudolf Kuenzli, and Gwen Raaberg, eds., *Surrealism and Women* (Cambridge: MIT Press, 1990); and Gloria Orenstein, "*Nadja* Revisited: A Feminist Approach," *Dada/Surrealism* 8 (1978): 91–106.

   Part of the accusation of misogyny is that the powerful, male figures of the movement suppressed participation by women (for example, Susan Suleiman's "A Double Margin," in *Subversive Intent*). The feminist response to this has spawned a literature devoted to recovering and celebrating the work of women surrealists. See "La Femme Surréaliste," the special issue of *Obliques* 14–15 (1977); Whitney Chadwick, *Women Artists and the Surrealist Movement* (London: Thames and Hudson, 1985); and Caws, Kuenzli, and Raaberg, *Surrealism and Women*.

4. See my *Passages in Modern Sculpture* (New York: Viking Press, 1977), 110–120.

5. Denis Hollier, "Surrealist Precipitates," *October* 69 (Summer 1994): 129.

6. Ibid.

7. Susan Rubin Suleiman, *Subversive Intent,* 115.

8. Ibid., 13; Suleiman is quoting Alice A. Jardine, *Gynesis: Configurations of Woman and Modernity* (Ithaca: Cornell University Press, 1985), 33–34.

9. Rosalind Krauss, "Corpus Delicti," *October* 33 (Summer 1985): 53.

10. Ibid., 71–72.

11. Suleiman, *Subversive Intent,* 116. Representative of the attacks on me is Rudolf Kuenzli's "Surrealism and Misogyny," in Caws, Kuenzli, and Raaberg, *Surrealism and Women,* 21–25.

12. Ibid., 16.

13. Ibid., 26.

14. Suleiman, *Subversive Intent,* 27.

15. Hal Foster, "Armour Fou," *October* 56 (Spring 1991): 96.

16. See Honor Lasalle and Abigail Solomon-Godeau, "Surrealist Confession: Claude Cahun's Photomontages," *Afterimage* (March 1992): 10–13; Laurie J. Monahan, "Radical Transformations: Claude Cahun and the Masquerade of Womanliness," in Catherine de Zegher, ed., *Inside the Visible* (Cambridge: MIT Press, 1996): 125–133.

17. Pierre Cabanne, *Dialogues with Marcel Duchamp,* trans. Ron Padgett (New York: Viking Press, 1971), 64.

18. I discuss this phenomenon of transitivism in Duchamp's work in "Marcel Duchamp ou le champ imaginaire," in my *Le photographique* (Paris: Editions Macula, 1990), 83–85.

Chapter 2: Louise Bourgeois: Portrait of the Artist as *Fillette*

1. Albert E. Elsen, *Origins of Modern Sculpture* (New York: Braziller, 1974), 74.

2. Breton, "Le Message automatique," *Minotaure* 3–4 (1933): 56.

3. Melanie Klein, *Contributions to Psycho-Analysis* (London: Hogarth Press, 1930), 242–243.

4. Bruno Bettelheim, *The Empty Fortress: Infantile Autism and the Birth of the Self* (New York: Free Press, 1972).

5. Gilles Deleuze and Félix Guattari, *Anti-Oedipus,* trans. Robert Hurley, Mark Seem, and Helen R. Lane (Paris: Editions de Minuit, 1972), 2.

6. Taped interview, cited in Deborah Wye, *Louise Bourgeois* (New York: Museum of Modern Art, 1982), 18.

7. Louise Bourgeois, *He Disappeared into Complete Silence,* introduction by Marius Bewley (New York: Gemor Press, 1947).

8. Wye, *Louise Bourgeois,* 20.

9. Ibid., 27.

10. Lucy Lippard, "Louise Bourgeois, From the Inside Out," *Artforum* 13 (March 1975): 31.

11. Georges Bataille, "Informe," *Documents* I, no. 7 (1929).

12. Roland Barthes, "The Metaphor of the Eye" (1963), in *Critical Essays,* trans. Richard Howard (Evanston: Northwestern University Press, 1972), 242.

Chapter 3: Agnes Martin: The /Cloud/

1. Lawrence Alloway, in *Agnes Martin,* exhibition catalog (Philadelphia: Institute of Contemporary Art, University of Pennsylvania, 1973), reprinted as "'Formlessness Breaking Down Form': The Paintings of Agnes Martin," *Studio International* 85 (February 1973): 62.

2. Ibid. Martin's text is published in Dieter Schwarz, ed., *Agnes Martin: Writings/Schriften* (Winterthur: Kunstmuseum Winterthur, 1992), 15.

3. Carter Ratcliff, "Agnes Martin and the 'Artificial Infinite,'" *Art News* 72 (May 1973): 26–27. For other discussions of Martin's work in relation to the abstract sublime, see Thomas McEvilley, "Grey Geese Descending: The Art of Agnes Martin," *Artforum* 25 (Summer 1987): 94–99; for her general placement within the category, see Jean-François Lyotard, "Presenting the Unpresentable: The Sublime," *Artforum* 20 (April 1982), and "The Sublime and the Avant-Garde," *Artforum* 22 (April 1984).

4. Robert Rosenblum's "The Abstract Sublime" (*Art News* 59 [February 1961]: 56–58), in which such comparisons are made for Pollock and Rothko, laid the foundation for later discussions in this vein.

5. In Schwarz, *Agnes Martin,* 15.

6. Ibid., 37.

7. Kasha Linville, "Agnes Martin: An Appreciation," *Artforum* 9 (June 1971): 72.

8. Ibid., 73.

9. In the formal notation of semiological analysis, the placement of a word between slashes indicates that it is being considered in its function as *signifier*—in terms, that is, of its condition within a differential, oppositional system—and thus bracketed off from its "content" or *signified*.

10. Hubert Damisch, *Théorie du /nuage/* (Paris: Editions du Seuil, 1972).

11. Ibid., 170–171.

12. Ibid., 69.

13. Alois Riegl, "Late Roman or Oriental?" in Gert Schiff, ed., *Readings in German Art History* (New York: Continuum, 1988), 181–182.

14. Quoted in Barbara Harlow, "Riegl's Image of Late Roman Art Industry," *Glyph* 3 (1978): 127.

15. Riegl, "Late Roman or Oriental?" 187.

16. For an important analysis of Kelly's recourse to chance, see Yve-Alain Bois, "Kelly in France: Anti-Composition in Its Many Guises," in *Ellsworth Kelly: The Years in France: 1948–1954,* exhibition catalog (Washington, D.C.: National Gallery of Art, 1992), 24–27.

CHAPTER 5: CINDY SHERMAN: UNTITLED

1. Lisbet Nilson, "Q & A: Cindy Sherman," *American Photographer* (September 1983): 77.

2. Richard Rhodes, "Cindy Sherman's 'Film Stills,'" *Parachute* (September 1982): 92.

3. Roland Barthes, *Mythologies,* trans. Annette Lavers (New York: Hill and Wang, 1972): 109–159.

4. Ibid., 125.

5. Rosalind Coward and John Ellis, *Language and Materialism* (London: Routledge and Kegan Paul, 1977), 43–44, 47.

6. In invoking the metaphor of the used car saleman and the buyer who does or doesn't look under the hood, I am perhaps implying that the myth's manipulation of signifiers and signifieds is somehow concealed. But it is important to emphasize that it is wholly visibile, out in the open. As Barthes says: "This is why myth is experienced as innocent speech: not because its

intentions are hidden—if they were hidden, they could not be efficacious—but because they are naturalized" (*Mythologies,* 131).

7. Another similar series—not sequential in a narrative sense but simply grouped around the same costume—is comprised of stills *#17–20.*

8. Judith Williamson, "Images of 'Woman,'" *Screen* 24 (November 1983): 102; she quotes Jean-Louis Baudry, "The Mask," *Afterimage* 5 (Spring 1974): 27.

9. Lisa Phillips, *Cindy Sherman* (New York: Whitney Museum of American Art, 1987): 14.

10. Roland Barthes, *S/Z,* trans. Richard Howard (New York: Hill and Wang, 1974): "What gives the illusion that the sum is supplemented by a precious remainder (something like *individuality,* in that, qualitative and ineffable, it may escape the vulgar bookkeeping of compositional characters) is the Proper Name, the difference completed by what is *proper* to it. The proper name enables the person to exist outside the semes, whose sum nonetheless constitutes it entirely" (191).

11. Phillips, *Cindy Sherman,* 8.

12. Arthur Danto, *Untitled Film Stills: Cindy Sherman* (New York: Rizzoli, 1990), 14.

13. Laura Mulvey, "A Phantasmagoria of the Female Body: The Work of Cindy Sherman," *New Left Review* 188 (July/August 1991): 137.

14. Abigail Solomon-Godeau, "Suitable for Framing: The Critical Recasting of Cindy Sherman," *Parkett* 29 (1991): 112.

15. Danto, *Untitled Film Stills,* 14.

16. Solomon-Godeau, "Suitable for Framing," 115.

17. Mulvey, "Phantasmagoria of the Female Body," 139.

18. Laura Mulvey, "Visual Pleasure and Narrative Cinema," *Screen* 13 (Autumn 1975): 6–18; republished in Laura Mulvey, *Visual and Other Pleasures* (Bloomington: University of Indiana Press, 1989): 15.

19. The sequence of texts in which Freud develops this scenario begins with "Infantile Genital Organization of the Libido" (1923), "The Passing of the Oedipus-Complex" (1924), and "Female Sexuality (1931). In the 1925 essay, "Some Psychological Consequences of the Anatomical Differences between the Sexes," the scenario takes a different form; it stresses the sense in which meaning does not arise in the presence of the visual field but is only retrojected on it as a result of a verbal prohibition: "When a little boy first catches sight of a girl's genital region, he begins by showing irresolution and lack of interest; he sees nothing or disowns what he has seen . . . It is not until later, when some threat of castration has obtained a hold upon him, that the obervation becomes important to him: if he then recollects or repeats it, it arouses a terrible storm of emotion in him and forces him to believe in the reality of the threat."

20. In their introductory essays, Juliet Mitchell and Jacqueline Rose present the development from the scenic event described by Freud to its subsequent semiological elaboration by Lacan. See Mitchell and Rose, eds., *Feminine Sexuality: Jacques Lacan and the Ecole Freudienne* (New York: Norton, 1982).

21. Mulvey, "Visual Pleasure," 14.

22. Stephen Heath, "Difference," *Screen* 19 (Autumn 1978): 89.

23. Mulvey, "Phantasmagoria," 141.

24. *Pictures* was the title of an exhibition organized in the fall of 1977 by Douglas Crimp for Artists Space, New York, which focused on work structured around the issue of replication, work that thereby could bring notions of representation into question. The five artists included Troy Brauntuch, Jack Goldstein, Sherrie Levine, Robert Longho, and Philip Smith. Crimp's connection to these issues continued and led to an essay that enlarged the circle of "pictures" artists to include Cindy Sherman. See Douglas Crimp, "Pictures," *October* 8 (Spring 1979): 75–88.

25. Douglas Crimp, "A Note on Degas's Photographs," *October* 5 (Summer 1978): 99.

26. Godard puts this in the mouth of Fritz Lang, in the film *Contempt*.

27. Ken Johnson, "Cindy Sherman and the Anti-Self: An Interpretation of Her Imagery," *Arts* (November 1987): 49.

28. Peter Schjeldahl, "Shermanettes," *Art in America* (March 1982): 110.

29. Mulvey, "Phantasmagoria," 142–143.

30. Jacques Lacan, *Ecrits,* trans. Alan Sheridan (New York: Norton, 1977), 290. Translation modified.

31. Ibid., 285.

32. These Lacanian "mathemes" appear in *Encore,* Lacan's 1972 seminar, and are published in *Feminine Sexuality: Jacques Lacan and the Ecole Freudienne,* 149. Here, the mathemes for the female subject are also given: $\overline{\exists\chi}\ \overline{\Phi\chi}$ (there is no x that is not submitted to the phallus); and $\overline{\forall\chi}\ \Phi\chi$ (not all x are submitted to the phallus). As Stephen Melville points out, it is from this matheme, which says the "same" thing as the mathemes for the male subject (there is an x that is not submitted to the phallus), but does so indirectly, without the same existential insistence, that Lacan derives the definition of the woman as "not-all": *pas-tout* (see n. 33 below, p. 355).

33. Stephen Melville, "Psychoanalysis and the Place of *Jouissance,*" *Critical Inquiry* 13 (Winter 1987): 353.

34. Freud's discussions of man's assumption of an erect posture as the first step toward culture and as making possible a sublimated visuality are in "Civilization and Its Discontents" (1930), *Standard Edition* 21: 99–100; and "Three Essays on the Theory of Sexuality" (1905), *Standard Edition* 7: 156–157. The gestalt psychological interpretation of the upright posture is from Erwin Straus, "Born to See, Bound to Behold: Reflections on the Function of Upright Posture in the Aesthetic Attitude," in Stuart Spicker, ed., *The Philosophy of the Body* (New York: Quadrangle, 1970): 334–359.

35. For the argument about Warhol's and Morris's reading of the horizontality of Pollock's mark, see my *The Optical Unconscious* (Cambridge: MIT Press, 1993); for the discussion of Ruscha's *Liquid Words,* see Yve-Alain Bois, "Thermometers Should Last Forever," in *Edward Ruscha: Romance with Liquids* (New York: Rizzoli, 1993). Both these readings are carried further in Yve-Alain Bois and Rosalind E. Krauss, *Formless: A User's Guide* (Cambridge: MIT Press, 1997).

36. The logic elaborated, for example, by Stephen Heath, slides from the phallus as signifier—as thus a wholly differential, nonpositive diacritical mark—to the phallus as form, which is to say gestalt or image. Heath marks this by replacing references to the phallus with the composite "penis-phallus," all the while acknowledging the problems this gives rise to. See Heath, "Difference," 55, 66, 83, 91.

37. Jacques Lacan, *Four Fundamental Concepts of Psychoanalysis,* trans. Alan Sheridan (New York: Norton, 1978), 96.

38. Mulvey, "Phantasmagoria," 143.

39. Victor Burgin, "Photography, Fantasy, Function," in *Thinking Photography* (London: Macmillan, 1982), 189–190.

40. In two instances of the publication of this work, different "interpretations" of its meaning are registered by means of the different ways the image has been printed. In *Cindy Sherman* (Munich: Schirmer/Mosel, 1987) the work's darkness and obscurity is respected; whereas in the Whitney Museum's catalogue for Sherman's retrospective, the image has been more highly exposed to force its values upward and thus to reduce its uncanny effect.

41. Lacan, *Four Fundamental Concepts,* 94.

42. See Roger Caillois, "Mimicry and Legendary Psychasthenia," *October* 31 (Winter 1984): 17–32.

43. Lacan, *Four Fundamental Concepts,* 99.

44. Ibid., 96.

45. Lacan, *Four Fundamental Concepts,* 99. Joan Copjec's essay "The Orthopsychic Subject: Film Theory and the Reception of Lacan" is an extremely important analysis of the distinction between film theory's "male gaze" and Lacan's *gaze as objet a.* Her understanding of this point in Lacan's argument diverges from mine, however, since she interprets the "itself" not as the subjectivity of the mimetic entity but as a kind of in itself that might lie behind the picture and which Lacan is, of course, refusing. But Lacan's use of *lui-même* rather than, for example, *en-soi,* makes her reading rather difficult. See Joan Copjec, "The Orthopsychic Subject," *October* 49 (Summer 1989): 69–70.

46. Lacan, *Four Fundamental Concepts,* 97.

47. That this function of the unlocatable gaze already conditions the subject's visual dimension in the same pattern of splitting, with the Imaginary already prefiguring the Symbolic, is articulated as follows: "Here too, we should not be too hasty in introducing some kind of intersubjectivity. Whenever we are dealing with imitation, we should be very careful not to think too quickly of the other who is being imitated. To imitate is no doubt to reproduce an image. But at bottom, it is, for the subject, to be inserted in a function whose exercise grasps it" (100). Jacqueline Rose addresses this visual, Imaginary prefiguration of the Symbolic, stressing its beginning in the rivalrous, aggressive aspects of Lacan's description of the mirror stage; see Rose, *Sexuality in the Field of Vision* (London: Verso, 1986), 180–181, 188, 192–194.

48. Sigmund Freud, *Leonardo da Vinci and a Memory of His Childhood,* trans. Alan Tyson (New York: Norton, 1964), 30–31.

49. Sigmund Freud, *Three Essays on the Theory of Sexuality,* trans. James Strachey (New York: Harper Torchbooks, 1962), 22, 44.

50. Mulvey, "Phantasmagoria," 150.

51. Ibid., 146.

52. Ibid., 148.

53. Ibid., 146.

54. Jacques Derrida, "The Purveyor of Truth," *Yale French Studies* 49 (1975): 38.

55. Ibid., 44.

56. Ibid., 60.

57. Ibid., 84.

58. Paul Taylor, "Cindy Sherman," *Flash Art* (October 1985): 79.

59. Lisbet Nilson, "Cindy Sherman: Interview," *American Photographer* (September 1983): 77.

60. Mira Schor, "From Liberation to Lack," *Heresies* 24 (1989): 17.

61. Hal Foster, "Armour Fou," *October* 56 (Spring 1991): 86.

62. Ibid., 96.

63. Mulvey, "Phantasmagoria," 139.

Chapter 6: Francesca Woodman: Problem Sets

1. Johannes Itten, *Design and Form* (New York: Van Nostrand Reinhold, 1975).

2. Although it is certain that many of the series referred to here were related to the kind of class assignment I am describing, it is not clear that all of them were. The opinions—and memories—of Woodman's classmates vary on the specifics of this issue. In all probability, however, *Charlie the Model* and *On Being an Angel* were not specific assignments but were only structured on the pattern of the problem set: a problem imagined and then turned into entirely personal account. The Foundation course given to all first-year students at RISD did use problem sets, although of a looser kind than those of the now-classic Bauhaus Vorkors.

3. Françoise Gilot and Carlton Lake, *Life with Picasso* (New York: McGraw-Hill, 1964), 51.

CHAPTER 7: SHERRIE LEVINE: BACHELORS

1. Michel Carrouges, *Les machines célibataires* (Paris: Arcanes, 1954).

2. Gilles Deleuze and Felix Guattari, *Anti-Oedipus,* trans. Robert Hurley, Mark Seem, and Helen R. Lane (Minneapolis: University of Minnesota Press, 1983).

3. Nietzsche, letter to Jakob Burckhardt, 5 January 1889, as cited in *Anti-Oedipus,* 86.

4. Marshall McLuhan, *Understanding Media* (New York: McGraw-Hill, 1964), 23, as cited in *Anti-Oedipus,* 241.